Wild truth

Bible Lessons

12 wild studies for junior highers, based on wild Bible characters

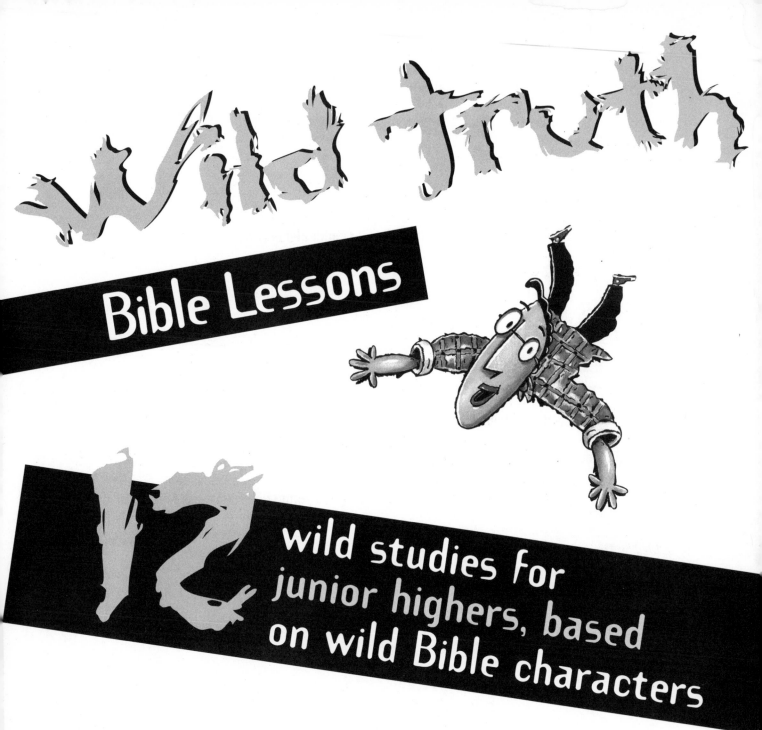

Wild truth

Bible Lessons

12 wild studies for junior highers, based on wild Bible characters

Mark Oestreicher

Youth Specialties

ZondervanPublishingHouse
Grand Rapids, Michigan
A Division of HarperCollinsPublishers

Library of Congress Cataloging-in-Publication Data

Oestreicher, Mark.
   Wild truth Bible lessons : 12 wild studies for junior highers / Mark Oestreicher.
      p. cm.
   ISBN 0-310-21304-5
   1. Christian education—Textbooks for young people. I. Title.
  BV1561.037 1996
  268'.433—dc20   96-22271
                      CIP

Edited by Tim McLaughlin
Cover and interior design by Patton Brothers Design
Illustrations by Krieg Barrie

Printed in the United States of America

99 01 02 / ML / 12 11 10 9 8 7 6

to Jeannie
thanks for tolerating my idiosyncrasies with such grace and humor—
I don't know what I'd do without you.

Acknowledgements

Thanks to—

Sam Fowler, Derrick Riggs, and Jeannie Oestreicher, who helped me brainstorm lesson outlines.

Kristi and Sam Fowler, who taught half these lessons as test cases.

The junior highers and Ground Zero staff of Lake Avenue Church, who let me try this material out on them.

Using *Wild Truth Journal* with the Lessons in This Book

The 12 Bible characters used in this book are among the 50 amazing characters who make an appearance in the author's book *Wild Truth Journal*—a spiral-bound journal that introduces junior highers to some of the most amazing people in the Bible. In each reading students explore the Scriptures for clues to the person's character, then discover how to apply these truths in their daily lives.

While the lessons here in *Wild Truth Bible* Lessons don't rely on *Wild Truth Journal* for teaching, their impact can be magnified with creative use of the journal. We've heard from resourceful youth workers throughout the country who've adapted *Wild Truth Journal* to work in their Sunday schools, Bible studies, small groups, retreats, and camps. Here are some of their best ideas, with suggestions for using them to support the lessons in *Wild Truth Bible Lessons*:

• **Coming Attractions.** If your students have their own copy of *Wild Truth Journal*, ask them to do the journal's lesson about the character on their own *before* you teach on the person. They'll be more familiar with the subject, your discussions will be more informed, and you can get to the meat of your lesson more quickly.

• **Return Visit.** Reinforce a lesson by asking students to do the journal's lesson *after* your teaching session. They'll stand a better chance of remembering the truths revealed—and of applying these truths that week.

• **Quiet Time and Again.** Distribute *Wild Truth Journal* to everyone at a retreat or camp, and ask students to use the journal's lesson in their daily time with God. Use *Wild Truth Bible Lessons* to shape your morning or evening messages. After the event students can continue using the journal in their quiet times at home.

• **Substitute.** Check out *Wild Truth Journal* when preparing your lesson—you may discover an alternative idea there that could work better for your group.

• **Extrapolate.** When you run out of characters in *Wild Truth Bible Lessons*, use the readings and questions in *Wild Truth Journal* for ideas in writing your own lessons on other Bible characters.

CONTENTS

INTRODUCTION

Of Stories, Scriptures, and Early Adolescents

I wrote *Wild Truth Journal* a year ago. It's a young-teen devotional that gets them into the Word of God. As I wrote it, I was struck again and again by the Bible's stories—after all, the Bible is replete with stories.

Early adolescents are only beginning to emerge from concrete to abstract thinking—a gradual process which can put a damper on their ability to deal with concepts of spirituality, theology, ethics, and morality.

Enter Bible stories, those ancient narratives that are actually made to order for today's junior highers. Bible stories are utterly concrete—real people in realistic situations, with just enough adventure, heartache, and gore to appeal to junior highers. Yet they point to principles of life that are as relevant as they are eternal. In other words, stories—in particular, Bible stories—help young teens transfer concrete people, actions, and places into abstractions that can affect their own behavior.

That's what *Wild Truth Bible Lessons* is all about. Ideally, you can use it *with Wild Truth Journal*. (See page 6 for more on this.) But you can teach this collection of lessons for junior highers just fine without *Wild Truth Journal*.

Each lesson contains four sections. Most good curricula follow, however loosely, the good old Larry Richards structure of HOOK, BOOK, LOOK, and TOOK (get the group interested together in the subject, check out what the Bible says about the subject, take your best guess at what the Bible passage means, then figure out how to take the meaning home and apply it to one's life). You'll find these same four components in each of the *Wild Truth Bible Lessons*:

> **Jump Start** is an attempt to bring your group together, into focus, while introducing the topic. Most of these are fun.
>
> **Getting the Point** lays out the basic teaching of the lesson.
>
> **Flashback** looks at a lesson learned from the life of the Bible character, whose story reinforces and builds the truth you've already presented.
>
> **Fast Forward** is simply concrete, practical application.

I don't have to meet you to know that you are among the finest people on earth for spending time with and investing yourself in junior highers. Ministering to them is a strategic, critical mandate in today's church—despite the fact that this is among the least visible, lowest-rewarded, and most overlooked ministries in Christendom. Thanks for caring for some of the most special people God made—young teens. I hope this book helps you to that end.

—MARK OESTREICHER

 **Kid King** *Josiah, on influencing others*

Bible passage: 2 Kings 23:1-3

GOALS

Students will—

- *Understand their ability to influence people in good ways or bad ways.*

- *Choose a specific way they will influence someone toward right living in the next week.*

 **JUMP START**

Designfluence

Create a big competition between two teams (boys against girls, seventh grade against eighth grade, left side of room against right side of room, etc.). Ask the first team to send two contestants to the front of the group. Blindfold one of the contestants, and give her the chalk or marker.

> **You'll need—**
> - copies of **Designfluence** (page 12), cut into quarters
> - chalkboard, whiteboard, or butcher paper with markers
> - blindfold

Say to your group: We're going to have an "influencing" contest.

Then give the other contestant one of the designs from **Designfluence** (page 12—either enlarge designs using a photocopier or project them with an overhead projector). Ask the student holding the design to describe it to the blindfolded student, who then attempts to draw it on the butcher paper or whiteboard. No touching or physical help is allowed—only verbal instructions.

After the first pair finishes, invite a pair from the other team to do the same task using the next design.

Then go through one more round per team. Finally, review the work of each team, having the kids cheer for their own contestants' work. Choose a winning team.

Say to your group: This team was a little better at influencing each other.

 **GETTING THE POINT**

Good and Bad

Ask for three volunteers. As you blindfold one of the volunteers, tell her that her job is to navigate an obstacle course by following the instructions of her teammates. After the blindfold is in place, quickly form a simple obstacle course using a few randomly placed chairs or other objects. Then whisper to the unblindfolded students their roles—one is to be a good influence, and one is to be a bad influence.

> **You'll need—**
> - chairs or other obstacles
> - blindfold

On "Go!" the two advice givers start shouting directions to the blindfolded student. That student attempts to get through the course as quickly as possible.

After the course has been completed and you're done bandaging all the bruised shins, get the kids talking.

Say to your group: We're all surrounded by good and bad influences every day. Can you name some

osiah was one of the very few kings of either Israel or Judah (he was of Judah) who "did what was right in the eyes of the Lord." Crowned as an eight-year-old when his father was assassinated, he was 26 when workers unearthed the Torah in the temple of the Lord—which triggered a spiritual reform like Judah hadn't seen for centuries. With the words of the Law ringing in his ears, Josiah cleaned house, big time. When he was done, you couldn't find an idol, pagan altar, or pagan priest anywhere in the land. And—here was the real mark of Jewish revival—he reinstituted the Passover nationwide.

good influences junior highers experience? Can you name some bad influences junior highers experience?

After they offer suggestions, say: *Just as we are influenced by other people and things, we are also always influencing people. Can you think of a time when you influenced someone?*

Wrap up this section by saying: *You have at least one choice to make all the time: will you influence people toward God and good decisions, or away from God and good decisions?*

Influence Questions
Continue your discussion of influence with the following questions:

• *If you were the blindfolded person in the obstacle course we just did, how would you have known who to listen to?*

• *What are different ways a person can be influenced? (by physical force, suggestion, example, etc.)*

• *If you could influence anyone in the world, who would it be and what would you influence him or her to do?*

• *Describe the last time you influenced someone on purpose.*

You'll need—
• no materials

• *What are some ways that junior highers can influence people toward bad choices?*

• *What are some ways that junior highers can influence people toward good choices?*

• *Who do you have the ability to influence?*

FLASHBACK

Joey's Influence

Pass out copies of **Josiah's Influence** (page 13), a "spontaneous melodrama." That is, you (or a student) read it, and the actors (who volunteer on the spot, no rehearsals) act out what you read and repeat dialogue— with melodramatic flair. If your group has 20 or more students, ask for 10 volunteers. Use fewer students in smaller groups.

You'll need—
• *Bibles*
• *copies of Josiah's Influence (page 13)*
• *pencils*

The same volunteers can act out all three versions; urge them to really ham it up. Before each version, reassign the new roles to the actors. In version three, make sure the students you cast as the goobers are not actual goobers in real life. Get the audience to react with oohs and ahhs, hisses and boos at the appropriate times.

Once all three versions are complete, applaud the acting ability of your volunteers, assure them that you will soon see them Off Broadway, and let them sit down. Now ask your students to open their Bibles to 2 Kings 23:1-3 and read the same story. Their job is to choose the version of **Josiah's Influence** that's most accurate and to draw a big star on it.

A note about translations: although the *Living Bible* is often very helpful with junior highers, it doesn't work as well for this exercise as the *New International Version*, which (in my opinion) best translates these episodes that demonstrate how Josiah influenced his people.

By the way, the third version of **Josiah's Influence** is the correct story.

Action Plan!

Photocopy **Action Plan!** (page 14) on card stock so the kids can put them in their Bibles and take them home intact (though you're probably dreaming if you think that *any* paper product would make it home in one piece). Pass out half-sheet copies of **Action Plan!** Your students should all have pencils from the previous exercises—and if they're normal junior high students, they've done hundreds of dollars of damage to chairs, walls, carpeting, and bodies since you last used the pencils.

You'll need—
• *pencils or pens*
• *cut copies of Action Plan! (page 14)*

Although the instructions on **Action Plan!** are self-explanatory, make no assumptions with junior highers. Explain that they're to devise a concrete plan of action for influencing someone in a positive way this week. Ask your students to quietly work on their own for a couple minutes. (Quietly...yeah, right.) Then ask if a few would share their plans of action with the whole group. Be sure to affirm those who share.

Close your time in prayer, asking God to give your students the courage to follow Josiah's lead and influence people toward good choices and God this week.

DESIGNFLUENCE

(see instructions, page 9)

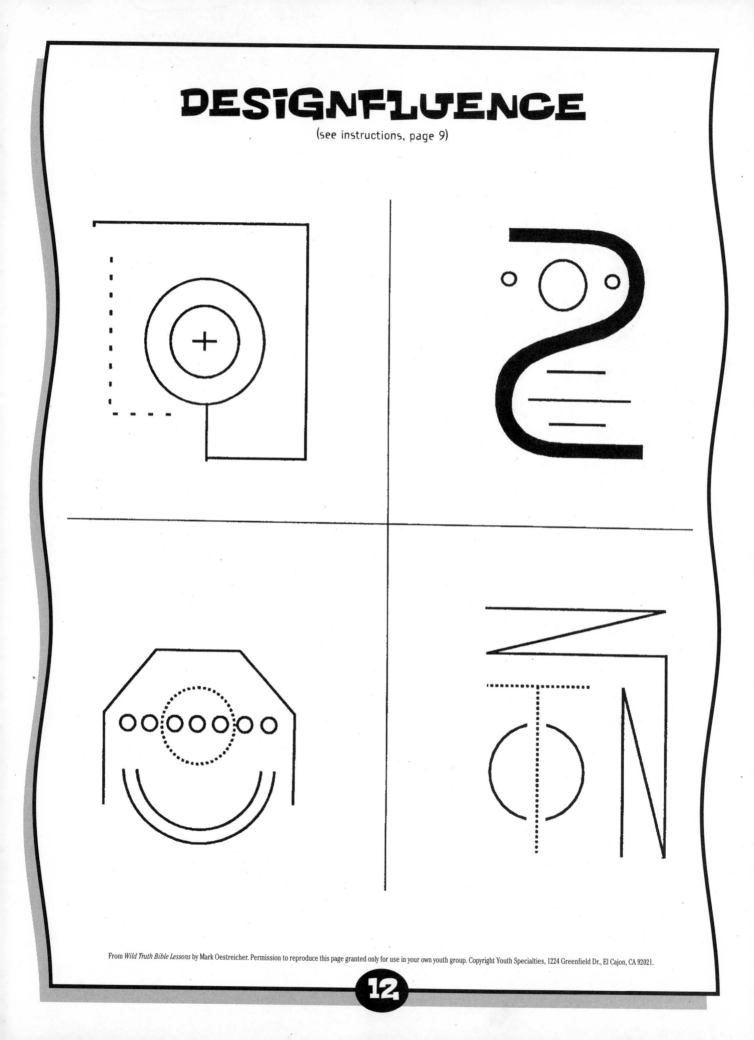

JOSIAH'S INFLUENCE

Scene: Josiah was king in Judah. Not a wimpy king with no real authority, but a king in a time and nation when everyone did whatever the king said to do. Now Josiah wanted to serve God; but the only copy of the Bible had been lost in the temple. When it was found, Josiah learned how far off track he and his people were from the way God wanted them to live. And he did something about it!

Version 1
JOSIAH'S TRICKLE-DOWN APPROACH

Cast: *Josiah; a bunch of priests*

Josiah was really bummed that he and his people weren't doing what God wanted. So he called a meeting with all the priests. The priests came to the meeting whispering and questioning what was going on.

Josiah said, "Shut up and listen!"

The priests were shocked that the king would talk to them that way. They all gasped in unison. One even had the boldness to ask, "Did your mother teach you to speak that way?"

Josiah ignored the priest and said, "We found the Bible. And you guys aren't instructing us right. Now read this thing and get it straight." With that he stomped out of the room and ended the meeting.

Version 2
JOSIAH'S COMMAND

Cast: *Josiah; a couple priests; a couple important people; a couple not-so-important people; Guido*

Josiah was really bummed when he found out how out-of-line he and his people were. So he called together a huge meeting. He asked everyone to come—priests, important people, and not-so-important people. Once they were all gathered, they all said, in unison, "What's up, Kingy?"

Josiah did a cool little king-dance up to the microphone and said, "From now on we're going to live by the book—God's book. And anyone who doesn't will meet my friend Guido." Josiah's bodyguard Guido flexed his muscles and did a few muscle-beach poses.

The people gasped in horror. Then they all said, in unison of course, "Whatever you say, Joey!"

Version 3
JOSIAH'S MODELING COMPANY

Cast: *Josiah; religious people; normal people; big-time goobers*

Josiah was really bummed when he found out he and his people weren't living the way God wanted them to live. So he called together a great big meeting. Everyone was invited—religious people, normal people, even big-time goobers. When they all gathered, they said in unison, "What is it, O King, that thou wouldst have us to do for thine own most powerful self?"

Josiah stepped up to the microphone and said, "Boy, you all talk really funny. Anyway, here's the scoop, people. I'm making a commitment to God, in front of you all, that I'm going to live for him." Then he stepped back from the mic.

The people all looked bewildered for a few moments, poking each other and saying, "Huh?" Then, one at a time, they all shouted out, "I'm gonna live for God, too!"

END

WILDPAGE

ACTION PLAN!

What's one thing you could do this week to influence someone you know in a positive way? Be specific!

Whom you'll influence	What you'll do	When you'll do it

WILDPAGE

ACTION PLAN!

What's one thing you could do this week to influence someone you know in a positive way? Be specific!

Whom you'll influence	What you'll do	When you'll do it

Wise Guy
the King of Good Decisions

Solomon, on wise decisions

Bible passage: 1 Kings 3:16-28

GOALS

Students will—

- *Be encouraged to make good decisions.*
- *Identify a decision they have to make this week and list the consequences of different choices.*

JUMP START

Would You Rather?

Read the following questions and ask students to answer by moving to one side of the room or the other. Explain to the kids that you'll point to one side of the room for one answer and the other side of the room for the other answer. (Just remember to actually *do* this when you read the questions.) What you're doing is creating opportunities for decision making.

You'll need—
- *no materials*

- Would you rather graduate from high school or skip high school and become a successful TV star?
- Would you rather get your nose pierced or your eyebrow pierced?
- Would you rather be an identical twin or an only child?
- Would you rather discover a cure for the common cold or be the President?
- Would you rather lose your sense of smell or your sight in one eye?
- Would you rather eat a raw cockroach or a cooked monkey?
- Would you rather have the superpower to fly or the superpower to be amazingly strong?
- Would you rather cliff dive or walk a tightrope?

- Would you rather be 20 and homeless or 90 and wealthy?
- Would you rather live where it's always 110 degrees, or where it's always 20 degrees?*

As the students are making their way back to their seats...

Say to your group: *We all make tons of decisions every day. Some of them are no big deal, but others have huge consequences.*

What Do They Do?

Preview the two video segments discussed below and cue them up before the meeting: *Raising Arizona* to 14:35, and *Tombstone* to 41:10.

Ask your group how good they are at guessing what other people will decide in a given situation. Then tell them you're going to check their ability to guess well.

Important note, if you want to keep your job it'd be best to show only the clips that are recommended here.

You'll need—
- *TV and VCR*
- *the videos* Raising Arizona *and* Tombstone

The author does not guarantee the appropriateness of scenes that immediately precede or follow the clips described here.

Before you play the *Raising Arizona* clip, explain to the kids that this is a comedy in which a couple is

*For hundreds more discussion starters of this sort, see *Would You Rather...?* by Doug Fields (Youth Specialties, 1995).

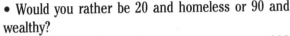

Who would have guessed that it would be the son of Bathsheba, *of all David's wives, who would succeed his father to the throne of Israel? Yet Solomon was as renowned for wisdom, wealth, and peace in the land as his warrior father was for military conquests. His astute ruling in the dispute between two prostitutes, both of whom claimed motherhood of an infant,* established his reputation for wise administration of justice.

Solomon, on wise decisions

unable to have a baby and so decides to steal one. This scene shows the Nicholas Cage character attempting to choose a baby.

Play the segment, then pause the video immediately after Nicholas returns to the car empty-handed, and the female says, "Don't come back here without a baby."

Ask your group: *What do you think he'll do?*

Focus the discussion on decision making. Young teens often find it easier to discuss the decisions of others rather than their own decisions.

Play the video from where you left off, to show what the man actually does (to 18:58, a little over four minutes of tape).

Then on to *Tombstone*, an action-western. Explain that the two men are total enemies—noted gunslingers who've killed many men and would not hesitate to kill another. But they've never met each other until this moment.

Play the clip, pausing the video immediately after Johnny Ringo finishes his gun showmanship. Ask those who've seen this movie not to respond to the next question.

Ask your group: *How do you think Doc Holiday will respond?*

Play the video from where you left off, to show how Doc Holiday actually responds (to 43:02, nearly two minutes of tape).

GETTING THE POINT

Little Decisions, Big Consequences

The two stories on **Little Decisions, Big Consequences** (page 18) illustrate how decisions that may seem mundane or small can still have big results. Sometimes these results are good and sometimes bad. Read the stories together as a group, or just read them to

the class yourself, then ask your students if they've ever made a decision that they thought was small, but it ended up having huge consequences. It would be great if you had a story of your own to tell.

You'll need—
• *Little Decisions, Big Consequences* (page 18)

Decision Questions

Continue your discussion of decisions with the following questions:

• *What's the best decision you ever made?*

• *What's one of the worst decisions you ever made?*

• *What's one of the worst decisions you heard about, that someone else made?*

• *What's the last big decision you made?*

• *What's a decision you need to make right now that you're having a hard time deciding what to do?*

The Baby-Sitter and the Gerbil

Ask for three volunteers to help with some acting. Make sure that at least two of the three are students who can ham it up. They'll be acting the roles of little kids, and the drama (okay, so the term is used *very* loosely) will be much more funny if they play their parts with gusto.

Give the three volunteers copies of the script for **The Baby-Sitter and the Gerbil** (page 19). You be the narrator yourself. Have the actors just read their lines and act them out

You'll need—
• *4 copies of The Baby-Sitter and the Gerbil (page 19)*
• *Bibles*

as well as they can, since there's been no rehearsal time. Suggest that they use little kid voices and attitudes.

Tell the audience you don't have any props, and they'll just have to use their imaginations.

After the skit is over, have everyone clap for your wonderful actors. Then ask if this story sounds familiar to anyone—if you have any kids who grew up in the church, they may really enjoy pointing out that it's basically a story from the life of Solomon.

Ask your students to turn in their Bibles to 1 Kings 3, and read verses 16-28 together.

Ask your group:
- *Why was Solomon's decision so wise?*
- *What makes a decision wise?*
- *Why do people make bad decisions?*

Consequence Analysis

Distribute copies of **Consequence Analysis** (page 20) to your students, and make sure they have something to write with. Explain that they're going to get two cracks at analyzing the consequences of specific choices—one time for an imaginary case study, and one time for a real decision they need to make.

Look together at the top half of **Consequence Analysis**.

You'll need—
- *copies of* **Consequence Analysis** *(page 20)*
- *pencils*

Point out that Derek has a choice about whether or not to dye his older sister's hair orange while she's sleeping. Have kids suggest the possible choices, and have everyone list them in the squares marked choice 1, choice 2, etc. If your students dream up more choices than there are room for

(there are only four spaces on the handout), they might have to eliminate some right away. (You'd think there aren't that many possible choices—but never underestimate the cavernous complexities of the junior high mind.)

After everyone's listed *at least* two possible choices (to dye or not to dye), ask them to list possible consequences below each choice. In fact, it wouldn't be a bad idea to ask the group, "What is a *consequence*, anyway?" This way you'll know if everyone's tracking with you.

After you've finished the top half of the page together, instruct your kids to complete the bottom half on their own. Have them fill in an actual decision they have to make this week, then list possible choices and consequences. Tell them that for some decisions, one of the consequences might be that the choice is opposed to God's teaching. For other decisions, it's as simple as choosing the option with the most desirable (or least undesirable) consequences.

Circulate amongst your kids to see if they need help. Some will probably struggle with identifying a decision they need to make, so here are some idea starters:
- Whether or not to complete a certain homework assignment.
- Whether or not to go to a party that will probably be fun, but might have some bad stuff going on at it.
- How much TV I should watch this week.
- How many times I should read my Bible this week.
- Whether or not I should invite a friend to youth group.

After it seems most have completed the task, ask if any want to share what they've written. Don't force anyone to share, but encourage those who do.

Close your time with prayer, asking God to give you all wisdom to make good decisions, especially with the specific decisions everyone wrote down.

LITTLE DECISIONS, BIG CONSEQUENCES

Rush to Port

The Titanic, when it was built, was considered invincible. It would never sink, its builders said. But late on the night of April 14, 1922, Captain Edward J. Smith became concerned that the ship—on its maiden voyage—was behind schedule. He was determined to get the ship to New York Harbor on time. In order to do this, he ignored the warnings of potential icebergs in the area and sped the ship up to its top speed. By the time he saw the huge iceberg in the ship's path, it was too late to do anything about it. More than 1,500 people, including the captain, died that night. Only 715 people, mostly women and children, survived.

The National Peach Basketball Association

In 1891 James Naismith's boss in the physical education department of Springfield College told him to come up with a team sport that could be played indoors during winter. Naismith decided to use a soccer ball because it was easy to catch, and asked the janitor to nail some wooden boxes to the gymnasium's balcony railing. The janitor didn't have any wooden boxes, so he found some old peach baskets. The first-ever game of basketball was played in Dr. Naismith's gym class, and the score was 1-0. The funny thing is, no one thought of cutting the bottoms out of the peach baskets—so they had to get a ladder to get the ball every time it went in the basket.

THE BABY-SITTER AND THE GERBIL

Cast:
Narrator
Jimmy (about five years old)
Bobby (about seven)
Baby-sitter (a junior higher)

Narrator: We take you to the bedroom of five-year-old Jimmy. His next door neighbor Bobby is spending the night. Bobby's seven. Jimmy and Bobby have one thing in common—they both have gerbils. They love to get together and watch their gerbils play. Tonight as they were going to bed in their sleeping bags, Bobby—who's not very bright—thought it would be a neat idea to have his gerbil, Muffin, sleep in his sleeping bag with him. There were many problems with this idea, the greatest of which was that when Bobby rolled over after about an hour of sleep, Muffin became a gerbil pancake. Bobby snuck over to Jimmy's gerbil cage and traded his own nonbreathing style gerbil for Jimmy's healthy version, named Puffy. Jimmy woke up and caught Bobby in the act, and all three of them, Jimmy, Bobby and Puffy quickly descended the staircase to the living room where the baby-sitter was watching TV.

Jimmy: He stole my Puffy!

Bobby: Did not! This is my Muffin!

Jimmy: That's not your Muffin, that's my Puffy! I saw you switching them!

Bobby: Liar, liar, pants on fire!

Jimmy: *(crying)* I want my Puffy!

Baby-sitter: What in the world are you two talking about?

Bobby: Jimmy's gerbil died, and now he's trying to take my Muffin!

Jimmy: That's not true! Big stupid Bobby squished Muffin, and now he's trying to steal Puffy! Oh, Puffy! *(Jimmy tries to reach out for Puffy, but Bobby swats him away)*

Baby-sitter: Okay, stop it! *(pointing)* Bobby, over there...Jimmy, over there. Now put the gerbil here *(pointing to imaginary table in front of him or her)* If you two can't decide whose gerbil this is, I've got a solution. I'll just take this big ol' kitchen knife and cut this thing in half—that way you can both have half of Muffin or Puffy or whoever this is.

Bobby: Sounds fair to me—cut away!

Jimmy: *(crying louder now)* No, no, just give Puffy to Bobby. Bobby can have her. Just don't cut her in half.

Baby-sitter: I think I can tell who's gerbil this really is. Bobby, we'll be having a little talk with your mother when she gets home. *(Bobby starts crying. Jimmy scoops up Puffy and smiles)*

END

CONSEQUENCE ANALYSIS

Derek's Decision:
Should he dye his older sister's hair orange while she's sleeping?

Choice 1	Choice 2	Choice 3	Choice 4
consequences	consequences	consequences	consequences

Your Decision:
_____

Choice 1	Choice 2	Choice 3	Choice 4
consequences	consequences	consequences	consequences

Donkey Boy, the Red-Faced Rider

Balaam, on responding to embarrassment

Bible passage: Numbers 22:21-33

GOALS

Students will—

- *Understand that there are good and bad ways to respond to embarrassment.*
- *Decide how to respond to embarrassment in three case studies.*

JUMP START

No Rules Game

This is one game my youth groups have played a lot, and it inevitably mutates into embarrassing situations. *But they're never so embarrassing that the game would be inappropriate.* Beware: this wild game could become a classic in your group, too.

You'll need—
- *no materials*

Tell your kids that this game has no rules until they create them. The object of the game is to follow all the newly made-up rules, so that you can avoid the consequences.

Have your students get in groups of five to eight kids. If this is all the larger your entire group is, that's okay—just have one group, and the game will still work fine.

Have each group sit in a circle. The oldest person in each circle gets to create the first rule. The rule can be anything they want it to be, like—

- No crossing your legs.
- You can't use the word *the*.
- You must yell *Yes!* after everything you say.
- No looking at the clock.

In addition to creating a rule, they must set a con-

sequence for breaking the rule. These can also be almost anything (within reason), like—

- If you break the rule, you have to stand and sing the national anthem.
- If you break the rule, you have to go to another group and bark at them like a dog.

After the first rule and consequence have been set, the play is passed clockwise, with each person in the circle adding a rule and a consequence. Don't stop after one time around the circle—just keep adding rules and consequences.

The whole time the game is being played, all players must watch all other players, trying to catch them breaking a rule. If caught, the rule breaker must submit to the consequences. If carrying out the consequences involves leaving the group for a moment, play continues while they're gone. And when they get back, no one is obligated to fill them in on any new rules and consequences.

Eventually, the game breaks down into hilarity, when no one can keep up with the quantity of rules and rule breakers.

This game will inevitably create some embarrassing moments. Ask kids about this after the game.

This has got to be one of the weirdest narratives in the Bible. Balaam was a free-lance voodoo practitioner of sorts—a hired gun who, for the right price, would curse the payee's enemies. Case in point: the Midianite king Balak summoned Balaam to use his services against Israel. On the way, there occurred the well-known incident of the talking donkey. And when Balaam finally opened his mouth to curse Israel, out came blessing instead. Yet later he was apparently responsible for serious immorality in Israel—with serious consequences for both him and Israel.

GETTING THE POINT

Embarrassing Moments

Continue your discussion on embarrassing moments by describing one of *your* most embarrassing moments. It would be best if your memory came from your teen years. (Teacher of the Year awards will be given to those who can actually list one from their *junior* high years.) Make sure you include in your story how you responded to the embarrassment.

After you've reminisced aloud, ask a couple students to share some of their embarrassing moments. Don't rush this part—kids enjoy this topic and will have lots of stories.

Responses

Have your group brainstorm different ways to respond to embarrassment. These should be general responses that apply to embarrassing situations in general, not specific reactions to stories just told. For example:
• Pretend nothing happened.
• Pout.
• Hide or run away.
• Get violent.
• Start crying.
• Laugh at yourself while thinking, "I'm the biggest scum-doggy on the face of the earth..."
• Shrug it off.

Write down the reactions suggested by students on a chalkboard, whiteboard, or overhead projector (a sheet of butcher paper and a marker work fine). What's important is getting the list of ideas up in front of the kids.

After you've got a whole list brainstormed, go through them one at a time and do two things: First, have everyone act out the response simultaneously. When you first suggest this, some kids will think you've lost your mind. The nonparticipatory, I'm-too-cool boys will certainly ignore you. But don't let it phase you—this can be fun. (If it's not, there's always room for workers in the children's ministry.) If you ham it up, chances are the kids will get into it, too. So if the response is "pout," get that lip out there as far as it'll go, and make some loud pouty noises—whimper, even. The idea is to make light of the different responses people have to embarrassing moments.

After you've acted out the response as a group, ask your students to judge the response as a "good" response or a "bad" response. Tell them that on the count of three, they should register their opinion by shouting "Good response!" while holding both thumbs up, or "Bad response!" while pointing both thumbs down.

After acting and judging each response, talk to your students for a few minutes about good responses...

Say to your group: *We always have a choice how we respond in these awful situations. But often, our responses just make the situation worse. The best possible response is "live and learn." As hard as it might seem sometimes, there's nothing we can do to change an embarrassing situation once it's occurred. So we might as well make the best of it. If you can learn to laugh at yourself, people will laugh with you, not at you. The worst thing you can do, however, is to pretend it doesn't matter to you, but underneath, to allow the situation to ruin your self-image. Embarrassment is part of life! Let's look at a Bible character who didn't handle embarrassment very well.*

Donkey Boy

Have your junior highers turn in their Bibles to Numbers 22:21-33. You, of course, have the book of Numbers memorized, and will be able to quote the whole passage...in reality, it may have taken you a second to remember that the book of Numbers has any stories at all.

Read the story of Balaam to your class, emphasizing the key points of the story. While your students' Bibles are still open...

Ask your group:
- *Who was Balaam with?* [some princes]

- *Why did who he was with make his situation more embarrassing?*
  [he really wanted to impress the princes]

- *Why was Balaam embarrassed by his donkey's actions?* [it looked like he didn't know how to control his animal—like your puppy going to the bathroom on a neighbor's carpet]

- *How did Balaam respond to the embarrassment?* [anger and violence—he yelled at his donkey and beat it]

- *What did it take for Balaam to understand why his reactions to embarrassment were wrong?*
  [the donkey spoke, and God revealed the angel to Balaam]

What Would You Do?

Distribute copies of **What Would You Do?** (page 24) to your students, along with something to write with (crayons, eye-liners, pieces of soft cheese, whatever). Read through the three embarrassing situations, then ask each student to write a specific response to each. Make sure they write their

own answers *before* you open it up for discussion (junior highers have a big-time tendency to say, "Yeah, what she said.") What you're aiming for is to have kids to think up their own applications.

Close with prayer, asking God to help them react in ways that will honor him when they get caught in embarrassing situations.

WILDPAGE

WHAT WOULD YOU DO?

That Warm, Wet Sensation

You drank a 32-ounce cup of Coke about an hour ago, during your lunch period, and have really had to go to the bathroom ever since. All of a sudden your teacher says something that makes everyone totally crack up. You're laughing your head off when you realize you are experiencing a warm sensation in your pants.

What would you do?

Hey, Is That a New Dance or Something?

Your parents let you attend your first-ever school dance. You're totally uncomfortable, because you don't know how to dance at all. And there seem to be all these unwritten rules about how to act—and you don't know any of them. Your friends finally convince you to get out on the floor for a group dance. Just as you start to decide that this is fun, you trip over your own foot and land face down on the ground—right as the music stops.

What would you do?

He Dropped Some Big Coin at Church

You're sitting in church and you're having a real hard time paying attention. You normally sit with your family. But today your mom let you sit with all your friends. So you're all in the back row. Some kids are passing notes and whispering. But you've actually been trying to listen. Unfortunately, you're tired and hungry and can't stay focused. Some lady is singing a hymn while the offering plates are being passed around, and she sounds just awful to you. Then your friend sitting next to you passes you something, and you make a quick grab for it without really knowing what it is. Well, it's the offering plate—awkward and heavy with the entire contents of some eight-year-old's piggy bank—and before you know it, the plate has slipped from your hand. Those 263 pennies make a ferocious racket when they hit the ground and scatter and roll (your church isn't carpeted). It seems like every head in the church turns around and glares at you.

What would you do?

Timothy, on living for God while still a young teen

Bible passage: 1 Timothy 4:12

GOALS

Students will—

- *Understand that they don't have to be adults to really live for God.*
- *Choose one thing to do this week to "go for it" with God.*

JUMP START

Impersonations

Ask for volunteers to come forward for two sets of impersonations. First have three or four kids impersonate a little child. A creative junior higher will have the group howling with this.

You'll need—
• *no materials*

After a few little kid impersonations, have a few students offer impersonations of an adult. Now this can be a little dangerous, for you never know what junior highers will do with an assignment like this. It could be interesting to see your students' depictions of how they see adults. And prepare to see yourself unflatteringly portrayed.

Make sure you have everyone give a big round of applause to every impersonator.

Ask your group: What are some of the nonphysical differences between little kids and adults?

Can't Wait

Read the following list of activities and decisions that junior highers often look forward to. Have kids rate their anticipation of them by their posture:

If they feel *"I could care less,"* they should slump over in their seats with their arms dangling down.

If they feel *"I can wait,"* they should just hunch over a little bit.

If they feel *"I'm looking forward to that,"* they should stand up.

If they feel *"I can't wait!"* they should stand up and wave their arms in the air.

Here are the activities:
- dating
- being done with school
- having kids
- picking your own classes
- driving
- setting your own curfew
- living on your own
- making all your own decisions

You'll need—
• *no materials*

Ask your group: What other things are you looking forward to?

You may get an occasional snicker out of this question, as seventh-grade boys eye each other and communicate telepathically: *Sex!* Depending on your church, it might be better to get this out in the open by just adding it to the list above. But you make the call.

There are virtually no "Timothy stories," except the brief I.D. that Luke gives of him in the book of Acts: a reputable disciple, Jewish mother (and a believer), Greek father. Paul picked him up in Lystra, Timothy's home—and that started at least several years of the young disciple's membership in Paul's traveling entourage. Later Timothy assumed the pastoral leadership of the church at Ephesus—a ticklish situation (what pastorate isn't?) that his apostolic mentor helped him navigate via a pair of letters to the young pastor.

GETTING THE POINT

Tombstone

While passing out copies of **Tombstone** (page 28), explain that an epitaph is a statement made after someone is dead that summarizes the person's life.

Tell your students to write an epitaph for themselves on the tombstone. Explain that it should be what they'd want it to say if they died a year from today.

In case kids don't understand, rephrase the assignment...

You'll need—
• copies of **Tombstone** (page 28)
• pens or pencils for everyone

Say to your group: If you die one year from today, what would you want people to remember about this year in your life?

Give students a few minutes to work on their own. (But heed your audience: if your junior high group includes any kids from aboriginal cultures, suggesting they discuss their death could be considered rude.) Ask if a few kids will share their epitaphs. Don't allow any comments like, "Oh yeah, like anyone would ever say that about you!" (Which means that you probably shouldn't make such comments, either.)

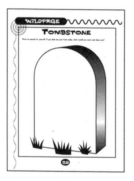

Ask your group:
• *Why do people think you can't do anything until you're an adult?*
• *Is there anything you can't do for God until you're an adult?*
• *What would it take for you to really go for it with God right now?*

FLASHBACK

Timmy Rebus

Say to your group: Timothy was one of the early church leaders. But he was kind of young. In fact, people weren't always too sure about him leading a church because he was so young. So Paul wrote him a letter and told him, among other things, how he should deal with the issue of his age.

Then pass out copies of **Timmy Rebus** (page 29). Your kids should still have their pencils or pens from the last exercise, and by now they've probably whittled them into toothpicks or used a pen shaft to perform an emergency-though-unneeded tracheotomy on an unsuspecting friend. Nonetheless, tell them they can work in pairs to try to solve the rebus. For junior highers who are creative conceptual thinkers, this will be a fun challenge. For others, this may be impossible. It's okay if they don't all get it. Let them struggle with it for a while, then have the whole group go through it together. The answer—a paraphrase of 1 Timothy 4:12—is this: *Don't let anyone look down on you for being young. Instead make your speech, behavior, love, faith, and purity an example for other believers.*

After you've figured the puzzle out together as a group, have them memorize the verse by coming up with fun hand motions for most words. For example, *Don't* could have a wagging no-no finger...*anyone* could be arms open wide...*look down* could be—well, looking down. Have fun with this. After you've figured out motions together, practice the verse with motions several times until everyone seems to have it memorized.

You'll need—
• copies of **Timmy Rebus** (page 29)
• pens or pencils for everyone

Adult Influence

Tell your kids it's time to put this lesson into practice—or at least to make plans to put it into practice.

Pass out half-sheet copies of **Adult Influence** (page 30). Your kids should still have pens or pencils from earlier use. Instruct them to follow the directions on the sheet, choosing an adult they will try to be an example to this week.

After a few minutes, have a few kids share their plans.

Close your group with prayer, asking God for courage to carry out these plans.

You'll need—
• *copies of Adult Influence (page 30), cut in half for each student*

TOMBSTONE

Write an epitaph for yourself. If you died one year from today, what would you want said about you?

TIMMY REBUS

Fill in the spaces with the words you think are represented by the pictures (one letter per line). Some pictures need letters added or subtracted before you write them down. For instance—

N + [cow] - C

means the word NOW. Get it?

The answer is a paraphrase of the Bible verse 1 Timothy 4:12.

___ ___ ___ , ___ ___

[DO crossed out]   L + [fly swatter] -N   N E 1

___ ___ ___   ___ ___ ___   ___ ___ ___ ___

[face spitting]   [down arrow]   [light switch ON]   U

___ ___ ___   ___ ___ ___ ___ ___ .

4   [BUZZZZ bee] +ing   [man & boy, arrow]

___ ___ ___ ___ ___   ___ ___ ___

[face, arrow] -ch+st+ [eraser] -br   [MAY calendar] +k

___ ___ ___ , ___ ___ ___

Y+ [spatula]   [face spitting]

___ ___ ___ ___ , ___ ___ ___ , ___ ___

[BUZZZZ bee] + [haystack] +v+y+ [spatula]   [heart]   Faith

___   ___ ___ ___   ___

&   [prrrr cat] + ity   N

___ ___ ___ ___   ___   ___ ___ ___

x + m + [apple] -ap   4   [boy & girl, arrow] -m

___ ___ ___ ___ .

[BUZZZZ bee] + [leaf] + rs

WILDPAGE

ADULT INFLUENCE

Your faith is an example to your peers. But it can be an example to grownups, too. Choose an adult in your life for whom you could be an example. Then write down what you can do this week to be that example.

Adult	What I can do	When I'll do it

WILDPAGE

ADULT INFLUENCE

Your faith is an example to your peers. But it can be an example to grownups, too. Choose an adult in your life for whom you could be an example. Then write down what you can do this week to be that example.

Adult	What I can do	When I'll do it

Flaky Sakes, the Thankless Bunch

The 10 lepers, on thankfulness

Bible passage: Luke 17:11-19

GOALS

Students will—

- *Understand that being a thankful person adds incredible happiness to life.*
- *Write a letter of thanks to someone and mail it or hand deliver it this week.*

JUMP START

Just Wanna Say Thanks

Arrange a competition between the girls and the boys by choosing a representative of each to compete in a little verbal match. Try to choose kids who have fairly good verbal abilities, if that's an option. This will help avoid a nonverbal student getting embarrassed in front of the other kids.

You'll need—
• *no materials*

Tell them there is an imaginary item they are both very thankful for. They are to take turns expressing, in words, how thankful they are for this item. The only catch is, they cannot use the word thankful, or any form of it. Instruct the girl to start. If they both come up with an equal amount of answers, they tie. If the girl thinks of a response, and the boy cannot think of another (within 15 seconds or so), then the girls win. Because the girl started, the boy will actually have to say an additional answer after the girl cannot think of one for the boys to win.

Thank-Off

Now include more kids in another contest. If you have a small class (12 or less), include everyone. If your group is larger, select six or eight volunteers to compete. Choose them to represent genders, grades, or schools, or you can simply choose them randomly.

Instruct them to say, "I'm thankful for ———." The word they are to provide must begin with the same letter that *ended* the word used by the previous player.

You'll need—
• *prize for the winner*

For example, if James says, "I'm thankful for *school*," then the next person must say, "I'm thankful for *lima beans*" or *Louisiana* or *lint*—anything that begins with *l* (the final letter in the word *school*).

This continues until contestants get eliminated for not producing an answer within 10 seconds. Students are also disqualified for using an answer previously given by anyone. Keep playing until you have a winner. If your kids are too good at this, and it seems you'll be playing until the return of Christ or the typical duration of your pastor's sermons (whichever is longer), simply shorten the response time to five seconds—or two seconds, if you want. If fact, you can do whatever you want with the rules—it's your class!

Think of a disease that debilitates victims socially as well as physically—AIDS, say. Now picture several men with AIDS, living in a city in the Bible Belt. One Saturday night on their way to a club they wander into a little Pentecostal church (only out of curiosity, for they are not especially religious people; one of them, in fact, is an atheist), a church where a healing service just happens to be going on. They get healed, get happy, and get out of there—to the nearest phone booth to call relatives and friends with the incredible news. At the door, though, one of the men stops, turns around, and walks back up the aisle toward the platform. He makes his way through the faithful who crowd the platform, waiting for their chance. He gets close enough to catch the healer's eye.

"Thanks," the atheist says. "I really needed that."

That's kind of what happened when Jesus healed 10 men of their leprosy, and only the Samaritan—a foreigner—returned to thank him.

By the way, don't get too discouraged if your kids are more intent on thinking up a word that starts with the right letter, than on gratefully recalling things they're thankful for.

Ask your group: If we can come up with that many things we're thankful for, how come most of us don't express our thanks very often?

GETTING THE POINT

Thankfulist

*Continue your discussion by asking: What are you **really** thankful for?*

After a couple minutes of responses, pass out copies of **Thankfulist** (page 34) and pens or pencils. Instruct students to write 10 things they're really thankful for down the left column—then, in the right column, why they're thankful for each of these things. Many of your students will get stuck after six or seven. Encourage them to think of 10 authentic answers (e.g., not "I'm thankful for peanut butter," unless, of course, peanut butter had somehow saved their life or played a crucial part in their conversion).

You'll need—
• copies of **Thankfulist** (page 34)
• pens or pencils for everyone

After all have completed their lists, ask a few kids to read some of their answers by selecting a number for them: "Candace, would you tell us your fourth answer? … Jake, would you read us your seventh answer?"

Say to your group: Some of the grumpiest, most unhappy people in the world are unable to express their thanks. Being a thankful person is not only a benefit to those you thank, but adds much happiness to your life.

Flaky Jakes

Below is a paraphrase of Luke 17:11-19. It's been rewritten with four key words: *thank(s)*, *leper(s)*, *heal(ed)*, and *Jesus*. These are cue words for audience participation.

Say to your group: We're going to look at some guys in the Bible who weren't very thankful—and one who was.

Now divide your group into four sections (the size doesn't matter—one kid or 50 kids per section will both work just fine). Assign a cue word to each group, and instruct them on the sound they should make when they hear that word:

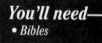

You'll need—
• Bibles

• *thank(s)*   Applause, cheering
• *leper(s)*   Shout "Unclean!"
• *heal(ed)*   Loud whooshing sound
• *Jesus*   Sing "Haaaal-le-lu-jah!" as in the first word to Handel's "Hallelujah Chorus"

Have each group practice their word and sound a couple times. Then read the story, pausing when you see the ellipses (...) long enough for each group to make their sound.

Jesus...was on his way to Jerusalem and was traveling along the border between Samaria and Galilee. As Jesus...was nearing a village, 10 lepers...met him. The lepers...stood a long way off from Jesus...and shouted, "Jesus...please heal...us!"
When Jesus...saw the lepers...he said, "Go to the priests and show them yourselves." So the lepers...went, and on the way they were healed....One of the former

lepers..., when he saw he was healed..., ran back to Jesus...and praised God. He threw himself at the feet of Jesus...and said in a loud voice, "Thank...you, thank...you, thank...you."

Jesus...asked, "Weren't all 10 former lepers...healed...? Where are the other nine? Would none of them say thanks...except you? Then Jesus...said to the former leper..., "Get up and go. Your faith has healed...you."

After you finish, you may want to show your students the actual passage in the Bible. (Without regularly taking our students into God's Word, we risk inadvertently teaching them that the Bible doesn't really have the answers to life, and that they are incapable of finding truth in the Bible themselves. So if you can, have your students read Luke 17:11-19 in their Bibles.)

Then ask your group:
• *Why do you think only one man returned?*
• *Why do you think the other nine didn't bother to thank Jesus?*
• *What are some of the things you forget to thank God for?*

Letter of Thanks

Hand out copies of the **Letter of Thanks** (page 35) or blank paper to everyone. If you collected their pens and pencils after the **Thankfulist,** pass them out again. I guarantee that if your students have had their pens or pencils since they completed that last task, at least one boy's **Thankfulist** now has in excess of 100 holes.

Tell your students they're going to have the opportunity to put this lesson into action—right now. They should write a letter of thanks to someone they've been neglecting to thank for a long time. Suggest that for many of them, this would be a great time to thank their parents for all they do. Other ideas:
• A teacher at school who shows extra care and takes time to make sure the students understand.
• A grandparent or other relative who always shows love.
• A former Sunday school teacher or coach who gave volunteer time to help them.

It's best if the kids don't just write letters to their best friends. Push them a little to write someone they wouldn't naturally write to, someone who would genuinely benefit from reading a thank-you letter.

Make envelopes available so kids can stuff their letters and write a name on the outside. Ask them to commit to either mailing or hand delivering the letter within the next week.

Close your time with group prayer. After you begin, ask students to pray one-sentence prayers in this format: *"Thanks, God, for ———."* Tell them they can pray as many times as they want. Don't force anyone to pray, but encourage them to all say at least one sentence. (If your group is big, you might want to break into groups of 10 or so for this final prayer.)

> **You'll need—**
> • *copies of Letter of Thanks (page 35), or blank paper and envelopes for every student*

THANKFULIST

What I'm thankful for	Why I'm thankful for it

Dave's Posse

David's mighty men, on doing outrageous things for God

Bible passage: 2 Samuel 23: 8-12,18-23

GOALS

Students will—

- *Understand that the Christian life is exciting when we step out of our comfort zones and do outrageous things for God.*
- *Select one outrageous thing they can do for God this week.*

JUMP START

Face Off

The goal here is to get kids used to the idea of moving out of their comfort zones—hence this crowd breaker, a game my kids play all the time. It conveniently, though obliquely, has to do with "zones"—a concept that can be vague to junior highers.

> **You'll need—**
> • no materials

Have kids pair up and stand face-to-face, about three feet apart. Tell them to put their hands against each other's, palm to palm, then separate their hands by a few inches. Their goal: to knock each other off balance. The first person to move either of their feet loses.

Students are allowed to hit only each other's hands, on the palms. They cannot push, pull, or grab each other. And they can't touch each other any place other than the palms of their hands. (If you don't make this last rule clear, some kids will probably be smacking each other on the side of the head.)

If you have enough time, you can have the winners regroup and play a tournament down to the final winner.

It's Outta My Zone

Say to your group: In that last game, you all stood in your own "zone" and tried to knock the other player out of their "zone." In a similar sense, we all have comfort zones, areas of behavior where we're comfortable. It's hard to step out of our comfort zones and do things that are uncomfortable.

Ask for nine volunteers to play **It's Outta My Zone** (page 40). If your group is smaller than nine, then adjust the game accordingly—either use less of the slips, or have some students participate more than once.

Ask a volunteer to pick a slip out of the hat (or whatever you use to hold the slips). After reading the instructions aloud, they must do one of two things: They may follow the instructions on the slip. Or they can yell, *"It's outta my zone!"* and pick another slip. If they take this second option, they *must* obey the second slip's instructions—they can't waive the second one. The first slip goes back in the hat.

When there's only one slip left, the game is over—because the person who draws it wouldn't have a choice.

> **You'll need—**
> • *It's Outta My Zone game slips (page 40), cut apart*
> • *something to hold the paper slips in (hat, bowl, offering plate)*

They were bad dudes, any way you cut it. Not the sort you'd want to meet in a dark alley. Or, for that matter, in broad daylight, even with the odds 20 to one against them. The way the Bible puts it, these guys were Super Heroes, King David's top warriors: the Three (Josheb-Basshebeth, Eleazar, and Shammah), their chief Abishai, and Benaiah, the head of David's bodyguard. Their feats were legendary—one killed 800 enemies in one encounter...another hewed down so many Philistines that, when it was over, he had to pry his hand off his sword handle...another skewered "a huge Egyptian" with his enemy's own spear. Schwarzenegger and Stallone, eat your hearts out.

When you've finished...

Ask your group:
- *Why did some of you choose to make a second pick?*
- *Was your second pick any better than your first?*
- *Were you out of your comfort zone?*
- *If you were, what did it feel like?*

GETTING THE POINT

What Is My Comfort Zone?

Distribute copies of **What Is My Comfort Zone** (page 41) and pens or pencils. Have students look over the lists of items on both sides. Then instruct them to connect each item with a line to either the comfort zone or somewhere outside the comfort zone.

After everyone has completed this task, ask a few volunteers to explain some of their answers.

You'll need—
- *copies of What Is My Comfort Zone? (page 41)*
- *pens or pencils for everyone*

Ask your group:
- *What makes something uncomfortable?*
- *Why would you be willing to try some uncomfortable things, but not try other uncomfortable things?*
- *Why do people differ in the boundaries of their comfort zones?*
- *What acts for God would be out of your comfort zone?*
- *Why or why not would you want to try something for God that's uncomfortable for you?*
- *What might some of the advantages be of doing something outrageous for God, even if it's uncomfortable for you?*

After discussion...

Say to your group: God has shown, both in the lives of people in the Bible, and in the lives of people today, that he will bless our efforts to do outrageous things for him. In fact, it's often only as we're risky and step out of our comfort zones that God will do amazing things. Let's look at some guys in the Old Testament who did some outrageous acts for God.

FLASHBACK

Wild Man Match-up

After you hand out copies of **Wild Man Match-Up** (the top part of the worksheet on page 42), tally up the cost of the damage your students have done with their pens or pencils since you last used them. Then ask your students to turn in their Bibles to 2 Samuel 23:8-12, 18-23, and read the passages.

You'll need—
- *copies of Wild Man Match Up (page 42)*
- *Bibles*

Next, have them use their Bibles to match the different mighty men with their outrageous acts.

Tell your kids not to bother with the bottom part of this Wild Page at this time.

After they've all completed the match-up, check answers as a group.

Ask your group:
- *Which act seemed most outrageous to you?*
- *How do you think it was possible for these guys to do some of these things?*
- *What would you do if you were Soldier #797, and Josheb-Basshebeth had just killed 796 of your fighting friends?*

Rate-a-rageous

Start this section by asking your students what the difference is between courage and "No fear." If necessary, explain that courage is moving forward into danger despite the fear you feel. "No fear," on the other hand, is simply denying that you have any fear. Tell your junior highers that God gets a lot more excited about courage than about "No fear."

You'll need—
• *no materials*

Now ask your students to rate the following outrageous acts for God. Tell them to hold up one to five fingers to show their rating: one finger means "not outrageous at all—this takes absolutely no courage, and I do this all the time." Five fingers means "massively outrageous—this would take tons of courage."

• *Stand up for truth in school.*
• *Share Christ with a friend.*
• *Be nice to someone who's not your friend.*
• *Sit with a loner at lunch.*
• *Give away some of your money to God's work.*

Explain to your group: Doing outrageous things for God doesn't mean you have to go kill 800 people with your spear. Doing an outrageous thing for God is as simple—or as difficult—as stepping out of your comfort zone to do something for him.

My Act

Direct students' attention to the bottom part of **Wild Man Match-Up** (page 42), to the box labeled "My Act." Assuming they still have their pens or pencils from earlier use, instruct them to pray silently for a minute, asking God what outrageous act he might want them to do for him, then write it down.

You'll need—
• *bottom part of Wild Man Match Up (page 42)*

After students are finished, use your judgment to decide whether or not to have a few students share their answers. If your kids have taken this pretty seriously, it might be better to keep their answers personal and private. But if you're not sure whether or not they really understood the assignment (and the lesson in general), field a few responses.

Close your time in prayer, asking God to give you the courage to step out of your comfort zones and accomplish these outrageous acts for him.

IT'S OUTTA MY ZONE
GAME SLIPS

Sing the National Anthem	Run around the room, flailing your arms and screaming, "I'm a nut case! I'm a nut case!"
Disco dance	Give a high-five to three people
Go sit down	Turn to the group and say, "Hi!"
Serenade someone of the opposite gender while on one knee (example: "You've lost that lovin' feeling…")	Quote the Bible verse, "Jesus wept"
Give your leader or teacher a big hug	Dance around like a monkey for 30 seconds

WHAT IS MY COMFORT ZONE?

Designate each item as in your Comfort Zone or out of your Comfort Zone by drawing a line to the appropriate area. The question isn't whether you'd be willing to do the items, but whether you'd be *comfortable* doing them.

bungee jumping off a 300-foot tower •

bungee jumping off a chair •

talking to a homeless person •

killing a spider •

wearing clothes that make me look fat •

having to share a bed with someone I don't know very well •

being asked a very personal question by a stranger •

speaking in front of 10 people •

speaking in front of 100 people •

speaking in front of 1000 people •

sharing my faith •

telling someone that I like them •

holding a snake •

telling my parents that I love them •

asking my parents about sex •

flying in a plane •

sitting by a stranger in a bus •

OUT OF MY COMFORT ZONE

Comfort Zone

OUT OF MY COMFORT ZONE

• ordering off a menu that's in another language

• baby-sitting for people I don't know

• solo performance in a musical (whether instrumental or vocal)

• confronting someone who's hurt me

• driving a car

• jumping off a high dive

• staying away from home for two weeks

• riding in a helicopter

• auditioning for a role in a play

• trying out for a sports team

• shooting a free throw in front of a full gym

• taking a final exam

• shaking hands with someone really famous

• reading the morning announcements over the school P.A. system

• praying aloud in a group

WILD MAN MATCH-UP

Look at 2 Samuel 23:8-12, 18-23, and match up David's mighty men with their outrageous acts.

Josheb-Basshebeth •

• killed 300 men with his spear

Eleazar •

• when his friends ran away, fought by himself until his hand froze to his sword

Shammah •

• killed 800 men in one battle

Abishai •

• went into a pit to kill a lion on a snowy day; also killed a giant with the giant's own spear

Benaiah •

• defended a field of beans by himself

MY ACT

Choose an outrageous act you can do for God this week.

What I'll do:

When and where I'll do it:

Whiny Bro
the Fair-Share Demander

The Prodigal Son's brother, on demanding your rights

Bible passage: Luke 15:11-32

GOALS

Students will—

- *Understand that demanding their "rights" has selfishness at its core.*
- *Identify a right of theirs they'd be willing to give up.*

JUMP START

Hot Potato

This old but still fun game sets the stage for exploring the idea of giving away, or giving up, something. You'll soon get to giving away one's rights—but right now, you're going to give away a hot potato.

If you have 15 kids or less, have them stand in a circle. If you have more students, divide them into groups of 10 or 15, and have each group form a circle. Give each circle a Ping-Pong ball or Wiffle ball or some other very light object. (Using a heavier object, like a rock or a lead pipe, could result in jail time for you.)

Now tell your kids they're going to play the ancient game of Hot Potato: they toss the ball to others in the circle. When the music stops, or the agreed-on 30 seconds is over, or whatever occurs that signals the end of a round—then whoever is holding the "potato" is eliminated.

Of course, there's a bit of an honor system in this game: if the ball is thrown to you, you *must* catch it—you just can't avoid it and let it fall to the ground. If the ball does fall to the ground, the person closest to it must pick it up and toss it.

> **You'll need—**
> - *a very light ball for every 10 or 15 kids (a Ping-Pong ball or Whiffle ball works well)*

Depending on how much time you have, run the elimination down to a final contest between two people.

After the game is over, introduce the topic.

Say to your group: *Your goal in that game was to give up the "potato." We're going to talk about giving up something else—your rights.*

I Give Up My Right to Breathe

Have kids stay in their circles of 10 or 15, although they can sit down for this game.

Pick one person in each circle to start the game by saying, "I give up my right to ——." Whatever kids say they give up must be something they can physically do *at that moment.* For example:

- I give up my right to have my right eye open.
- I give up my right to sit down.
- I give up my right to hang my arms at my sides.
- I give up my right to not have my teeth clenched.
- I give up my right to use my left leg to stand with.
- I give up my right to not cluck like a chicken.

Here's the catch: not only the student who made the statement must then and there give up that right—that is, do (or not do) an action—but *everyone* in the circle must do it. And as the next person and the next add more statements, all students add those actions to what they're already doing. As students are

> **You'll need—**
> - *no materials*

Some think that tradition has misnamed Jesus' story: instead of "The Prodigal Son," it should be called "The Prodigal's Brother," for the story is as much about the reaction of the responsible older brother, when his kid brother returned home after partying away his entire inheritance.

unable to think of a new statement or are unable to sustain all the actions from the previous statements, they are eliminated from the game.

GETTING THE POINT
How Hard Would It Be?

Say to your group: *Those were some pretty weird things to give up. Let's look at some things that might be a little harder for you to give up.*

Pass out copies of **How Hard Would It Be?** (page 46) and pens or pencils to each student. Instruct them to rate each right from 1 to 10 on how hard it would be to give up that right for the stated time (1 = it'd be a piece of cake to give up; 10 = it'd be totally impossible to give up).

After students have filled out their sheets, ask for some responses to a few of the items.

Ask your group:
• *What's a right?*
• *Who decides what's a right and what isn't?*
• *What happens when your rights conflict with the rights of someone else?*
• *What do you think the Bible has to say about our rights?*

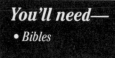

Say to your group: *In a minute, we're going to see someone in the Bible who struggled with this issue.*

At the Core

This simple object lesson illustrates what it means to have something at the core radiate out and affect the whole.

Hold up the apple for your class to see, and let kids see that it is a healthy apple. Ask them what determines if an apple is truly healthy or not. As you get answers, begin to pare the apple, gradually exposing the core.

When you've pared away everything *but* the core, explain that the core defines the apple: at the center of a

healthy apple, you'll find a healthy core. But a diseased core will never produce a healthy apple.

Say to your group: *The core of not giving up your rights is selfishness.*

Whiny Bro

The story of the Prodigal Son makes a fun spontaneous melodrama. Assign the various roles to kids in your group:
• Prodigal Son
• father
• older brother
• two or three pigs (or a whole herd!)
• servant

Read the passage straight out of the Bible (Luke 15:11-32). Before you begin, explain to your students that you realize most of them have heard this story many times, but you want them to watch the story through the eyes of the older brother.

For how to perform a spontaneous melodrama, see the suggestions on page 10, under "Flashback."

Once my volunteers used this passage as a spontaneous melodrama in their small groups of junior highers. I kept hearing thumps in one of the rooms a small group was meeting in, as if people were getting thrown against the walls.

Later I asked the leader what had been going on. "Oh, that," he said. "The pigs just got in a fight."

So after this dramatic pageantry of pig and pot roast is concluded...

Ask your group:
• *What was the older brother's complaint?*
• *If the older brother got his share of the inheritance also, why would he have any reason to be upset?*

• *Who does the father represent in this story? (God)*
• *What does God want to tell us about our rights through this story?*

FAST FORWARD

Cough 'Em Up

Distribute copies of **Cough 'Em Up** (page 47) to everyone. They should still have pens or pencils from when you used them earlier.

Ask your junior highers to fill in the two columns: six rights they feel are really rights, and six right's they'd like to think are rights, but are probably just selfishness. If kids are having trouble with the latter list, prime the pump with suggestions like these:
• My right to a room of my own
• My right to spend my money however I want
• My right to say what I want to say
• My right to be comfortable
• My right to have nice clothes
• My right to watch TV

After they've filled the page, ask them to look back over the list, especially the right column, and circle one thing they'd be willing to give up this week. Again, this might be really difficult for some kids. Push them a bit, explaining that the more we practice unselfishness, the less selfish we'll be. We have to learn how to give up our rights—because many of us have learned just the opposite for so long.

Close your time in prayer, asking God to give everyone courage to unselfishly give up their rights.

How Hard Would it Be?

Rate each of the following rights from 1 to 10 on how hard they would be to give up (1 = it'd be a piece of cake to give up; 10 = it would be totally impossible to give up).

How hard would it be for you to give up...

___ sleep for one night?

___ sleep for two whole days and nights?

___ TV for one afternoon and evening?

___ TV for a week?

___ TV for a year?

___ talking for a day?

___ talking for a month?

___ seeing your family for a year?

___ seeing your family for 10 years?

___ the ability to get out of bed for six months?

___ your sight for a week?

___ your sight for a month?

___ your sight for the rest of your life?

___ love and affection for a year?

___ your hair forever?

___ your thumbs for a month?

___ your house for a day?

___ your house for a month?

___ your current friendships forever?

Cough 'Em Up

List a few items in each box.

Rights that are really rights

Rights I'd like to think are rights, but are probably just selfishness

Now...circle one right, in either column, that you are willing to give up for one week, beginning today.

Moe's Mom the Cruise Director

Moses' mother, on trusting God in difficult situations

Bible passage: Exodus 1:22-2:10

GOALS

Students will—

- *Understand that God will take care of them in difficult situations.*
- *Make a commitment to trust God in difficult situations.*

JUMP START
Difficult Connections

This lighthearted mind-stretcher introduces the idea of something not so lighthearted for young teens today: difficult situations. And from all reports, adolescence today is a much more difficult situation in general for your junior highers than it probably was for you.

Distribute copies of **Difficult Connections** (page 53) and pens or pencils to each of your students. The instructions are quite simple. They are to draw three lines: one line to connect the two boxes labeled A, another line to connect the two boxes labeled B, and a third line to connect the two boxes labeled C. The three lines cannot cross each other at any time, cannot pass through a box, and cannot go outside the boundary lines.

Here, by the way, is the solution:

You'll need—
- *copies of Difficult Connections (page 53)*
- *pens or pencils*

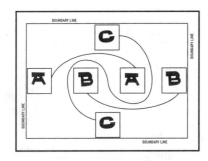

Let the kids work individually or with others if they prefer. After a few minutes, ask if anyone solved the problem. If someone did, have them share their answer. Otherwise, you share it.

Trust Me

Ask for three volunteers to leave the room. While they're out of the room, recruit two others to help you. One will need to snicker at just the right time, and the other will only need to quietly say, "Don't do it."

Bring the volunteers back in one at a time for a little test of their ability to trust. Place a chair facing your group and have the volunteer stand about two feet the side of it. Explain what you're going to do while you carefully blindfold her.

You'll need—
- *blindfold*
- *chair*

Say to your group: *I'm going to ask you to stand totally motionless for about a minute. During that time, I'm going to move that chair right behind you in position for you to sit on it. And when I say, "Sit now!" you should sit down without any hesitation. Okay?*

Ask the group to be totally silent also. Very quietly, trying to make absolutely no noise, move the chair into position. This is no time to be Youth Worker Of The Practical Jokes—make sure the chair is close to the back of the volunteer's legs, so when she sits she won't miss.

Jochebed was mother to a girl and two boys: Miriam, Aaron, and a little tyke who, simply by being alive, could've gotten her killed. Yet she risked death to keep her infant Moses alive—and thanks to an ingenious little plan she concocted with her daughter, she succeeded. Jewish history has never been the same. (Egyptian history had a dent put in it, too.)

While you're moving the chair, the two "plants" in the audience fulfill their roles: one snickers, and a moment later the other says almost in a whisper, "Don't do it..."

When the chair is in place and you've waited long enough to make the volunteer *really* nervous, say "Sit now!" Most will hesitate. Some will even reach their hands down behind them to see if the chair is really there. Very few will trustingly plop down on the chair.

If the volunteer *doesn't* hesitate or crouch before sitting, congratulate her on her trust, and have everyone applaud her. If she hesitates at all, ask her why she didn't trust your word that the chair would be in place.

Repeat the activity with the second and then the third volunteers.

 # GETTING THE POINT

Difficult Situations

By way of transition...

Say to your group: *First we did something that was kind of difficult—but it was only a puzzle, so it didn't matter if you couldn't figure it out. But when you get into a difficult situation in life, it sure seems like it matters a lot if you can't figure it out. God tells us he wants us to trust him when we're in difficult situations. Of course, he wants us to trust him all the time. But trust gets harder and harder when we're in difficult situations.*

> **You'll need—**
> • no materials

Next, read these three short stories to your kids. After each, have them comment on how difficult they think it would be to trust God to take care of the situation. Make them explain their answers—don't let them get away with just saying, "Yeah, it'd be hard..."

Nick's Nightmare

Everything seemed great—until last night. He knew his family wasn't perfect. But he sure didn't see this coming. Two days ago his parents told him they were probably going to split up. And last night he, his sister, and his mom moved out of their house into an apartment. But it didn't really sink in until he lay in the dark on the couch of the new apartment, trying to fall asleep, that his dad was staying all alone at the house. A realtor was com-

ing the next day, he had heard, to put the house up for sale, and then his dad would apparently move into an apartment, too.

How hard would it be for Nick to trust God in this situation?

Kara's Confusion

Kara had tried everything, and was still totally confused. A couple months ago, it had been too hard to tell Jenna the truth—so she had lied to her. Later, Kara finally told Jenna the real truth. She knew that Jenna would be upset at having been lied to, but she'd hoped that Jenna would at least appreciate being told the truth eventually. But Jenna was more than upset—for a month now, she hasn't taken phone calls from Kara or even looked at her in class. Kara's all but convinced she's lost her best friend forever.

How hard would it be for Kara to trust God in this situation?

Jino's Gym

He didn't have a clue what he'd done to start this. But it was obvious to Jino that his gym teacher really didn't like him. When Jino told his mom, she called the school and talked to the principal. The principal must have spoken to the gym teacher—because the situation only got worse. It's not that the gym teacher makes Jino do extra work or anything. He just glares at Jino like he'd be thrilled if Jino fell off the face of the earth. Jino's tried working harder, he's tried smiling and being nice—nothing works. And he doesn't even know what he did to make the teacher so upset.

How hard would it be for Jino to trust God in this situation?

My Story

Pass out blank pieces of paper and have students write stories about a time when they were in a difficult situation. Tell them to talk about trusting God, and about how God helped the situation (if they know). Make it clear that God doesn't always fix situations the way we'd like them fixed. So some of their stories may still seem unresolved, unfixed.

> **You'll need—**
> • blank paper
> • pens or pencils

Some kids will have a hard time coming up with a story. They've all experienced tough stuff of some sort. But some aren't willing to reflect on that; others will simply, in their unique junior high way, draw a blank. If you know your kids well, you can quietly remind them of episodes or situations. At least you can suggest general categories to help them think: trouble with a friend...trouble with a parent or both parents...a tough move or school change...trouble with a teacher...difficult peer pressure...confrontation with a bully.

After a few minutes, have a few kids share their stories. Ask the same question from the short stories: *How hard was it to trust God in that situation?*

The Desperate Mom

Say to your group: *I'm going to read you one more story. But this one's a little different. It's not about a junior higher in a difficult situation. It's about a mom—a desperate mom.*

Then read this modernized telling of the story of Moses' mother:

The rumors were everywhere. She was sure the secret police would come any hour now to her seaside town. She'd already received a phone call from her sister in the town of Torning that the secret police had been there. The sister told how she continued to hear the screams and cries of the mothers who lived all around her.

For months the leaders of Ruman—the country where she lived—had been grumbling about the growing number of Bansic baby boys. Bansic people were not Ruman natives, but refugees who had been allowed to settle in Ruman because they were a convenient source of unskilled labor. Actually, the Bansic

> **You'll need—**
> • Bibles

refugees were very skilled at a number of occupations. But the Rumans hired them only for the most menial of jobs and paid them accordingly—about a tenth of what most Rumans earned.

Now the government was getting nervous, because this wave of Bansic boys would one day be young men, and there would be more Bansic men than Ruman men. The government knew this would be trouble. How would they ever keep control?

So yesterday a motion passed in the Ruman Congress that the mother could hardly believe was true. All Bansic boys under five years old were to be killed within the next 48 hours. The mother had a son, Mason, only eight months old.

Desperate to find a solution, the mother soon realized there were none. She bowed her face to the ground, sobbing, and begged God to help her. Her deep faith gave her some comfort, but this situation was almost unbearable. As her weeping subsided, she again heard the constant, distant crashing of waves on the coast only a short walk from her house. The sea...

She stood up, calm at last, and knew what she must do. She spoke a few words to her daughter, whose eyes opened widely as she listened, but who nodded and immediately walked toward town. Then the mother went to their tool shed and found a can of tar her husband had purchased to seal leaks in their roof. With quick, deliberate strokes, she spread tar all over the inside of her baby's bassinet.

Almost numb now to feelings, she wrapped Mason tightly in his blanket and set him in the little homemade boat. She carried him down to the cove and walked into the water until it was shoulder deep. She murmured a prayer for God's blessing as she pushed the bassinet out into the current, which carried the bassinet quickly out into deep waters. By the time the mother reached the beach again, feelings had resurfaced, and she collapsed on the sand, unconscious.

Now about that time, the private yacht of the prime minister's daughter motored away from the dock for an afternoon cruise. She was disgusted with the child-death motion her father had made and the Ruman politicians had passed. As she sunbathed on the immense deck of her yacht, she

closed her eyes to doze. She opened them sleepily a few moments later, and found herself looking directly at—well, something bobbing in the swells a few dozen yards away from the yacht. She rolled over, called up to the captain, and askeed him to snag whatever it was and bring it in for a closer look.

Soon the bassinet was on deck, and she was astonished at its tiny cargo. It was clearly a Bansic baby—a Bansic male, at that. But Bansic or not, her heart was taken by him, and she decided then and there to have him as her own son.

Per her mother's instructions, Mason's sister was waiting near the dock when the yacht returned, pretending to sell vegetables from her basket to passersby—but alert and watchful. The prime minister's daughter stepped onto the dock—and the sister then saw the family baby blanket bundled in those aristocratic arms. She made her move, sweeping up her basket and walking up to the prime minister's daughter.

"I know a qualified Bansic nanny near here, if you're interested," she told the elegant woman—who agreed and arranged for generous payment on the spot.

Later that day a government car brought Mason to his own home, to be raised by his own mother. In spite of everything, God had answered her prayers in a way she never would have imagined.

Ask your kids if this story sounds familiar to any of them. Some will recognize it as the story of Moses' mother. Have them all turn in their Bibles to Exodus and read the original story from 1:22 to 2:10.

Ask your group: Why should we trust God in difficult situations?

Pick a Verse

Before your group meets, make enough **Difficult Situations** bookmarks (page 54) for all students. Copy them onto card stock, if you can. Your kids should still have pens or pencils from their earlier use.

Write the following references on your chalkboard, whiteboard, or overhead projector:

- Proverbs 3:5
- Philippians 4:13
- Romans 8:38-39

> ### You'll need—
> - one *Difficult Situations* bookmark per student (page 54)
> - *pens or pencils*
> - *Bibles*
> - *chalkboard, whiteboard, or overhead projector*

Now pass out the **Difficult Situations** bookmarks. Instruct your kids to look up all three verses (or do it together) and choose one that they think would help them trust God in difficult situations. Tell them to write the verse, or their own summary of the verse, on the top half of their slip or card.

After they've done this, ask them to take a moment to write, on the bottom half, a difficult situation they're involved in right now. If they're worried about privacy, let them know it's okay to use code or wording that someone else wouldn't understand if they glanced at the paper. And assure them that you won't ask them to share their responses with anyone.

Finally, ask your kids to spend a minute or two in silent prayer, making a commitment to God that they will trust him in difficult situations.

After prayer, suggest that they keep these bookmarks in their Bibles, or put them up in their bedrooms to remind them that God is worthy of our trust.

DIFFICULT CONNECTIONS

Use your pen or pencil to draw three lines: one line to connect the two boxes labeled A, another line to connect the two boxes labeled B, and a third line to connect the two boxes labeled C. The three lines cannot cross each other at any time, cannot pass through a box, and cannot go outside the boundary lines.

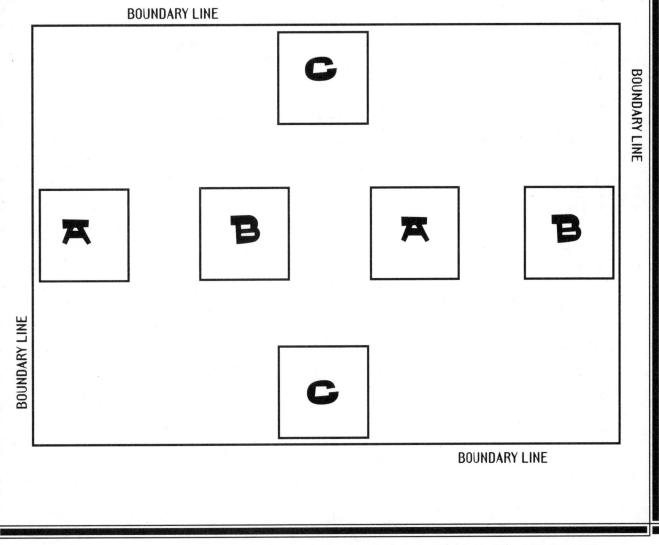

DIFFICULT SITUATIONS
bookmarks

My verse for difficult situations:

My present difficult situation:

My verse for difficult situations:

My present difficult situation:

My verse for difficult situations:

My present difficult situation:

My verse for difficult situations:

My present difficult situation:

Poor Mama, the Giving Queen

The poor widow, on giving

Bible passage: Mark 12:41-44

GOALS

Students will—

• *Understand that God is less interested in how much they give than in why they give.*

• *Choose a way they will give to God this week.*

JUMP START

Give Away

Create two to four teams, two kids per team (more teams for large groups, fewer for small groups). Tell the contestants that they will be completing the sentence, "We give you ——." They may fill the blank with anything *that they can literally give at that moment.* This could be anything from a coin to a look to a high five.

Teams are eliminated when they can't think of a new sentence within 10 seconds, or when they repeat something already said. If your kids are Rhodes Scholars in training, and it appears the game will last until your pastor's tie comes back in style— then limit the time allowed to five seconds (even two seconds if necessary).

Appoint one team to begin—and let 'er rip!

When the game ends, congratulate the winners with wild applause.

You'll need—
• *no materials*

Gut-Level Giving

Pass out copies of **Gut-Level Giving** (page 58) and pens or pencils to each student.

Say to your group: Now we're going to get down to some real giving

You'll need—
• *copies of Gut-Level Giving (page 58)*
• *pens or pencils*

stuff. *Let's find out what you're willing to give and what you're not willing to give.*

Instruct students to rate each item on a 1-10 scale, with 1 meaning it'd be super easy to give away, and 10 meaning it'd be almost impossible to give away.

Have kids work on their own for a few minutes. Then ask them to give responses to each item.

Ask your group: *What else would be really hard to give away?*

GETTING THE POINT

Giver's Anonymous

Read the following pair of stories about junior highers who gave. Use the questions at the end of each story to spur your class to analyze the person's motive for giving.

You'll need—
• *no materials*

New Release

Kevin was on his way to the music store. He was totally stoked! He'd wanted the new Frenetic Toads CD for weeks, and had finally saved up enough money to buy it.

As he neared the store, a homeless man caught

esus saw her drop a couple pennies into the temple treasury. Yet she was no cheapskate, Jesus pointed out to his disciples. *"This poor widow has put more into the treasury than all the others,"* he explained. *"They all gave out of their wealth; but she, out of her poverty, put in everything—all she had to live on."*

his eye. This guy was one of the saddest sights he'd ever seen. He wasn't even asking for money or anything—just sitting in a doorway looking like he'd lost all hope in the world.

Kevin thought for just a minute, then walked up the homeless man nervously.

"Hey mister," he said. "Can I buy you some lunch?"

The man looked up at Kevin in disbelief. "Pardon me, son?" he said.

Kevin took the man to McDonald's and spent $4.16 of his $20. More than once during their lunch, the man looked at Kevin with bleary eyes and said, "I think you're an angel that God sent from heaven." Kevin knew he wasn't an angel, but it sure felt nice that someone thought he might be one. Kevin walked home with not quite 16 bucks in his pocket. And no CD. That would just have to wait, he guessed.

Ask your group:
- *Why did Kevin do what he did?*
- *From puny to huge, what was the size of Kevin's gift?*
- *Would you have done the same thing?*

Heavy Loaf

For a month Amy's youth group had been collecting money for a Sudanese hunger project. They were all given little plastic banks shaped like bread loaves to put their spare change into during the month. On the final Sunday they were all to bring their banks in, break them open, and pour the contents into a big metal drum. Amy remembered the last time she'd seen this done, and how everyone had oohed and ahhed at the sound of all those coins dropping into the metal container from the banks of the people who'd saved a lot.

She was determined to be one of those people this year.

The important Sunday was here, but all Amy had accumulated in her little loaf were a few pennies and nickels. So she stuck a couple dollar bills in her pocket, and on the way to church stopped by a 7-Eleven—where she got 200 pennies to fill her loaf bank.

During her youth group time that morning, she hoisted her heavy bank and plunked in on a table in front of her. The sound was impressive—obviously weighty. And no one could tell it was only pennies inside. She carried the loaf up to the front like it weighed 50 pounds. And as she cut the loaf open and dumped the contents into the metal drum with the loudest possible clanking sounds, she put on her most impressive I-care-about-those-poor-starving-Sudanese-kids face and pretended not to notice the admiration of the group.

Ask your group:
- *Why did Amy do what she did?*
- *On a scale of puny to huge, what was the real size of Amy's gift?*
- *Amy and Kevin both gave $4.16. What was the difference?*

Dramarama

Depending on the size of your group, have students form teams of four to 10 kids each (at least two teams would be best, but you can have as many as you want).

Instruct the groups to open their Bibles to Mark 12:41-44 and read it together. Then tell them they have

five to 10 minutes to put together a short, one-to-two-minute drama based on that story. They can play the story literally, modernize it, perform it as a musical, deliver it as a daytime TV talkshow—whatever.

Circulate among the groups while they work, offering any help you can.

When time is up, pull everyone together to watch and enjoy each other's sketch. Be sure to encourage and applaud each group, no matter how rough their presentation might be.

Ask your group:
- *Why did the widow give everything she had?*
- *On a scale of puny to huge, what was the real size of her gift?*

- *Would you have done the same thing?*
- *What's Jesus teaching us, and the disciples, in this passage?*

My Gift to God

Ask your group: What are some different ways, besides giving money, that junior highers can give to God?

Possible ideas: being friendly to a lonely person, volunteering time to help in children's church, cleaning up around their house without expecting any payment or praise.

You'll need—
- *My Gift to God (page 59), cut in thirds*
- *pens or pencils*

After kids have suggested several ideas, pass out copies of **My Gift to God** (page 59). Your kids should still have their pencils or pens from the earlier part of this lesson.

Ask them to take a minute to pray silently, asking God what he wants them to give this week. Then instruct your group to write down a private commitment to God of something they'll give to him this week. They need to write what they'll give (money or something else) and when they'll give it.

Don't ask your kids to share their answers this time—it could easily go against the point of the lesson, and kids could end up like Amy in the story above.

Ask a student to close your time in prayer, asking God to give you all courage to follow through on your giving commitments.

GUT-LEVEL GIVING

Rate each item for how easy or difficult it would be to give away (1 being super easy to give away, and 10 being completely impossible to give away).

_____A $5,000 savings bond that you can convert to cash when you're 50

_____Your brother or sister

_____Front-row tickets to a concert by your favorite group

_____All your shoes except your oldest pair

_____A $20 bill

_____All your meals for one day

_____Your lunch money

_____A free round-trip ticket to anywhere in the world

_____Your favorite outfit

_____A presidential invitation to dinner at the White House

WILD GIFT

My Gift to God

My gift to God this week...

What I'll give:

When and where I'll give it:

WILD GIFT

My Gift to God

My gift to God this week...

What I'll give:

When and where I'll give it:

WILD GIFT

My Gift to God

My gift to God this week...

What I'll give:

When and where I'll give it:

Jonathan, on friendship

Son, the Friend of Friends

Bible passage: 1 Samuel 20:1-23

GOALS

Students will—
- *Understand that in order to have good friends, they need to be good friends.*
- *Choose one thing they will do this week to be a good friend.*

JUMP START
Know Your Friend

Begin with a little competition between the boys and the girls. Select a pair of friends from each team (a pair of boys that are friends and a pair of girls that are friends). Keep one boy and one girl in the room, and have the other boy and girl go out in the hall with an adult. Recruit a recorder, and give him or her a sheet of paper and a pen to write down answers.

You'll need—
- *one sheet of paper*
- *a pen or pencil*

Seat the remaining boy and girl up front. Ask them the following questions, and have the recorder write down the answers.

Ask your group:
- *What color are your friend's eyes?*
- *When was your friend's last hair cut?*
- *What's your friend's favorite school subject?*
- *Name a musician or band that your friend really doesn't like.*
- *What name would your friend pick for him or herself if he or she was the opposite gender?*

Now have the two kids in the hall come in, and have their teammates leave for the hallway. Do not discuss the answers to the first set of questions at this point. After the switch has been made, ask the new pair of competitors the following questions. Make sure the recorder writes down their answers.

Ask your group:
- *What's your friend's phone number?*
- *What is your friend's least favorite school subject?*
- *What is your friend's middle name?*
- *Name a musician or group your friend really likes.*
- *What occupation would your friend like to have when he or she is an adult?*

Now reunite the friends. Have them all stay up front while you ask the first set of questions to the second set of contestants—the individuals the questions were about—and vice versa (to the second set of contestants, for example, ask "What color are your eyes?"). After their response, the recorder reveals what their friend *thought* the answer was. Keep track of correct answers and whoop it up for the winning team.

Say to your group: *We all need friends. It's pretty lonely to go through life without friends. But sometimes it seems really difficult to find good friends. Sure, everyone has good friends sometimes. But everyone occasionally feels like they don't have any friends at all.*

His father, King Saul, accused him of hanging out with a traitor and usurper, but that didn't stop Jonathan from counting David a friend worth risking his life and royal future for. In the end, both Saul and Jonathan were killed in an ill-advised battle. Yet David later proved his love for his friend by giving a son of Jonathan, Mephibosheth, a place at the royal table for every meal—a kindness, David said, for the sake of his father Jonathan. (This, in contrast to the common practice of a new king slaughtering all members of the ex-royal family.)

GETTING THE POINT

Design-a-Friend

Distribute copies of **Design-a-Friend** (page 64) and pens or pencils to each junior higher.

Their mission, if they will accept it, is to draw an ideal friend. It shouldn't depict an actual friend, but the *perfect* friend. Explain that they might draw big ears to signify that the friend is a good listener, and things like that. They should write on the picture as much as they want, in order to explain their drawing. Tell them to list down the sides of the picture the qualities of this ultimate friend—what makes him or her a good friend?

Time Out

*D**id you know how rare and wonderful a person you are to teach junior highers? You are dear to God's heart, and to be highly esteemed. Others may think you're psychotic to work with kids this age, but God knows the truth—you are pouring your life into young adolescents who may be at their most critical stage of life.*

Give students a few minutes to work on their own. Then ask a couple of the junior highers to share their pictures.

Now ask your kids to look back over their pictures and circle the character traits that could be said about themselves. Prod them to be really honest, and not to circle an item unless it's really true of them much of the time.

Ask your group:
• *What's the number one most important quality of a good friend?*
• *Why is it so hard to find good friends?*
• *How do you find a friend?*
• *What's the worst thing a friend can do to you?*
• *How many really good friends can one person have before some of the friendships get a bit shallow?*
• *What are the names of some friends in the Bible?*

[Shadrach, Meshach, and Abednego; David and Jonathan; Ruth and Naomi; Jesus and John; the guys who lowered their lame friend through the roof]

FLASHBACK

Jon and Davey Readers Theater

Ask if anyone can tell some of the details of the friendship between David and Jonathan. Then ask for two volunteers to come read the parts of Jon and Davey in an impromptu readers theater. Give each of them a copy of **The Legendary Friendship of Jon and Davey** (page 65), and assign their roles. You read the part of the narrator (with a hidden-camera-type whisper: "We're here at Chez Weenie, where we've secretly replaced the hot dogs with dachshunds...").

The script is a summary of the 1 Samuel 20:1-23.

After reading the script together (you'll laugh...you'll cry...)—

Ask your group:
• *What made Jon and Davey's friendship a good one?*
• *What's loyalty?*
• *How does loyalty enter into this story?*
• *We don't see a lot of the story of Jon and Davey's friendship here. What other friendship qualities would you guess were in place already to make their loyalty to each other so strong?*

FAST FORWARD

Pick-a-Pick

Explain to your group that it's time to put this lesson into action. Pass out copies of **Pick-a-Pick** (page 66). Your kids should still have at least the remnants of the pencils you handed out earlier.

The sheet is self-explanatory. Just ask kids to—

• Pick a friend.

• Pick a friendship quality they can improve in that friendship. (Remember the traits of their ideal friend they jotted down earlier in the lesson? They can choose a trait from that list if they want.)

• Pick a plan to improve that friendship quality.

• Pick a time and a place this week that they'll put that plan into action.

If time allows, have a few kids share their plans.

Close your time in prayer, asking God to help you all be better friends, like he is a friend to us.

You'll need—
• copies of *Pick-a-Pick* (page 66)

WILDPAGE

PICK-A-PICK

• Pick a friend.

• Pick a friendship quality you can improve in that friendship.

• Pick a plan to improve that friendship quality.

• Pick a time and a place this week that you'll put that plan into action.

66

DESIGN-A-FRIEND

Draw the perfect friend. For example, you might draw big ears to show that your perfect friend would be a good listener. Point out all of his or her special friendship features similarly. List extra friendship qualities of this imaginary person down the sides of the page. In fact, write all you want on this page.

THE LEGENDARY FRIENDSHIP OF JON AND DAVEY

A readers theater for three

CAST:
  Narrator
  Davey
  Jon

NARRATOR: Jon and Davey have already been friends for some time. Davey's been chosen to be the next king. But Jon's dad, the present king, isn't too excited about this. In fact, Jon's dad pretty much wants to kill Davey.

DAVEY: Jon, I don't get it! Why's your dad so ticked at me? What have I done to him? I mean, he's trying to kill me!

JON: No way! He won't do it. Here's the deal: my dad doesn't do anything without confiding in me. So why would he hide this from me?

DAVEY: Your dad knows we're buds. So I'm sure he's just thinking, I can't let Jon know I'm gonna waste his friend—it would bum him out. But I'm telling you, Jon, there's only a step between me and death.

JON: Okay, then, tell me what to do, and I'll do it.

DAVEY: Here's the plan: I'm supposed to go to a big dinner party at your dad's place tomorrow night. I won't show up, and you tell him I had to go out of town for a family emergency. Watch his reaction. If it's no big deal to him, then I'm safe. But if me not being there totally hacks him off, then you and I will both know he wants me six feet under.

JON: Whoa.

DAVEY: Thanks for your friendship. I mean, really, if I'm wrong on this thing, then just kill me yourself!

JON: NO STINKIN' WAY! If I even thought for a second that my pop wanted you pushin' up daisies, don't you think I would have told you?

DAVEY: So who will come tell me if your dad goes ballistic?

NARRATOR: So Jon and Davey worked up a sneaky little plan that was pretty complicated. It involved shooting arrows into a field at different distances and all kinds of weird stuff. But it worked: Jon was able to let his friend Davey know that his dad did, indeed, want to kill Davey.

JON: God will protect you, I know it! And I love you, man!

END

PICK-A-PICK

• Pick a friend.

• Pick a friendship quality you can improve in that friendship.

• Pick a plan to improve that friendship quality.

• Pick a time and a place this week that you'll put that plan into action.

Peter, on God's forgiveness

Bible passages: Matthew 16:17-19; 26:31-35; 26:69-75
Mark 16:6-7
Acts 1:15-16; 2:14

GOALS

Students will—

• *Understand that God's forgiveness is always bigger than their sin.*
• *Ask forgiveness for a sin, then put it behind them.*

JUMP START

Forgiveness Bingo

Hand out copies of **Forgiveness Bingo** (page 70) and pens or pencils to each student. Tell them they'll be trying to get people to sign the different squares, thereby admitting that what's written in the square is something they've needed forgiveness for sometime during their lives. Each student's goal is to complete two rows in any direction—horizontal, vertical, or diagonal.

Be sure to add a rule that limits how many times the same person can sign someone's sheet. If your group has 20 or more kids, an individual can sign the same sheet only once. If you have 10 or fewer kids, relax the rule so kids can sign the same sheet two or three times.

Without much more instruction or stalling, get

> **You'll need—**
> • *copies of*
> *Forgiveness Bingo*
> *(page 70)*
> • *pens or pencils*

them mingling with a decisive "Go!"

Clarify rules as you proceed, if necessary. Keep track of the first three people to finish, checking their sheets to make sure they completed it correctly. Then stop the game and congratulate the winners.

GETTING THE POINT

Three Pictures of Forgiveness

Ask for two volunteers to play the parts in **Three Pictures of Forgiveness** (page 71). One will play God, the other will play the junior higher.

Ask them to act out the first scene. Then before they go on to the second scene...

Ask your group: How is this like God's forgiveness? How is this unlike God's forgiveness?

Then have the actors proceed with scene 2 (with a time-out for pondering the same question), and the same sequence for scene 3.

In scene 1 God is distracted and doesn't give a hoot. He doesn't know what's going on in the life of the junior higher. He grants forgiveness only to get rid of him.

> **You'll need—**
> • *2 copies of the script*
> *Three Pictures of*
> *Forgiveness (page 71)*

Peter was a blue-collar laborer. He got his hands dirty making a living. The open Sea of Tiberius (as the Sea of Galilee was then called) was no carpeted, well-lit office. He spent his fishing days (and nights) among hard-working, hard-drinking, hard-talking men. So Peter just may have had some experience at cursing before the night of Jesus' trial, as he denied knowing the man he had followed for three years. Yet in one of the most scandalous displays of grace depicted in the Bible, Jesus later forgave the impetuous disciple and reinstated him—this time as the leader of Christ's followers.

In scene 2 God is ready to grant forgiveness, but punishes the junior higher by withdrawing his love until she earns it back.

In scene 3 God is loving, honest, and forgiving.

Close this section with a couple more remarks about forgiveness:

Say to your group: God will <u>always</u> forgive us. He promises us that there is nothing we can do that he won't forgive. But that doesn't mean we can just sin like crazy and expect it won't be a big deal. First of all, there are consequences to a lot of our sins. Even though God forgives, he very rarely removes the consequences of our sin. If you murder someone, God will forgive you, but you'll still go to jail.

Secondly, God's forgiveness requires both confession and repentance from us. We need to confess—tell God our sins. This helps us to really be aware of them. And we need to repent—which means we need to change our actions. In other words, we're not really asking forgiveness of God if we plan on running right out and doing the same sin again in 30 seconds. God will forgive the same sin again and again, but when we ask forgiveness, we need to intend to change.

The Saga of Pete's Forgiveness

Say to your group: Now we're going to look at an amazing example of God's forgiveness. It's found in the life of Peter.

You'll need—
• Bibles, or copies of *The Saga of Pete's Forgiveness* (page 73)

Either pass out copies of **The Saga of Pete's Forgiveness** (page 73), which has the complete text of the Bible passages printed on it, or have kids turn their Bibles to the first passage.

Tell your junior highers they'll be looking at five different parts of Peter's story to see how God's forgiveness weaves through the whole thing.

First, have everyone read Matthew 16:17-19. This is where Jesus renames Peter. Explain that the name Peter means *rock*. So when Jesus says he'll build his church "on this rock," he is suggesting that, in addition to building the church on the rock of the Gospel, Peter himself will be a significant stone in the church's foundation.

Ask your group: Why is this a big deal? How would you feel if you were Peter?

Move on to Matthew 26:31-35. In this passage Jesus predicts that Peter will say he doesn't know Jesus. Peter, of course, strongly denies that this will ever happen.

Ask your group: How would you feel if you were Peter now? Why do you think Jesus bothered to tell Peter he would do this?

With your students, look a little farther into the chapter (verses 69-75) where Peter does deny knowing Jesus.

Ask your group questions like these:
• *How did Peter feel?*
• *How would he have felt knowing that Jesus had predicted this?*
• *Did Jesus know that Peter would deny knowing him when he named him "the rock," and said he'd build his church on Peter?*
• *What does it say about forgiveness that Jesus knew this about Peter and still had huge plans for him?*

Now move on to Mark 16:6-7. Before the kids read the passage, explain that Jesus has been crucified, buried, and risen, and three female followers of Jesus have just been to the tomb and found it empty. In this passage the angel tells the women to go tell the disciples that Jesus is risen. Interestingly, the angel singles Peter out: "Go tell the disciples *and Peter*."

Ask your group:
• *Who does the angel tell the women they should go tell?*
• *Since Peter was one of the disciples, why do you suppose that God had this angel single out Peter—as if to make especially sure that he got the message?* [Possible answer: Peter was having a major pity party, feeling totally awful about his sin. God wanted him to know, specifically, that Jesus was alive.]

Finally, look quickly at Acts 1:15-16 and Acts 2:14. These two short passages demonstrate that what Jesus had predicted was actually occuring: Peter was assuming a major role in the foundation and leadership of the church.

Ask your group: Why would Jesus still have Peter play such an important role in the beginning of the church just a few weeks after he'd denied even knowing Jesus? [Possible answer: because God had totally and completely forgiven Peter—his sin was part of his past]

God to reveal to them a sin that they need to ask forgiveness for. Then ask them to write this sin, in actual words or some sort of code words, on their cups.

When everyone is done writing, have them place their cups rim-down on the ground. Then, on the count of three, have everyone stomp their cups. The noise is great (especially on an uncarpeted surface; the burst has been known to spike pacemakers in the Senior Saints Sunday school class next door). Even better than the noise, though, is the symbolism.

Explain to your group that those sins are gone. Just like Peter's sin of denying Christ was totally removed, so are their sins when they take advantage of God's great endless forgiveness.

Close your time in prayer, thanking God for his forgiveness.

Then pick up the cups—or else face the wrath of the church custodian. (If you haven't yet faced the wrath of the church custodian, you can't really call yourself a youth worker.)

Cup Stomp

Environmental dilemma ahead! For this exercise, Styrofoam cups work better than paper cups—they're easy to write on with pens, make a great popping noise when stepped on, and kind of explode all over the place if you stomp them just right. Perfect for junior highers. But Styrofoam, as everyone knows, is not environmentally friendly. So you make the call.

You'll need—
• *cups*
• *pens or pencils*

Hand out a cup (paper or Styrofoam) and a pen or marker (pencils don't work for this) to each student. Ask them to take a moment to pray silently, asking

FORGIVENESS BINGO

Get signatures of others who have needed forgiveness for these acts or attitudes at one time or another. Complete *two* rows in any direction—vertical, horizontal, or diagonal.

stole something	laughed at a dirty joke	beat up my brother or sister	ignored God
lied to a friend	used profanity	yelled at my parent	spread a rumor
cheated on a test	lied to my parent	saw a movie my parent said I couldn't see	held a grudge
gossiped	had a complaining attitude	skipped school	hated someone

Three Pictures of Forgiveness

Cast:
  Jr. higher
  God

SCENE 1

Jr. higher: God?

God: Not now, I'm busy.

Jr. higher: But, uh, God...O Great One?

God: Oh, all right. I guess if you're going to bother calling me O Great One. What is it?

Jr. higher: I sinned.

God: Gee, what's new?

Jr. higher: And I need forgiveness.

God: Yeah, don't you all. What did you do?

Jr. higher: Don't you already know?

God: Yeah, yeah. But regulations say you gotta name it.

Jr. higher: I, um, lied to my parents.

God: Yer gonna fry in hell! No, just kidding. Okay.

Jr. higher: Okay?

God: Yeah, okay, now leave me alone.

SCENE 2

Jr. higher: God?

God: Yes?

Jr. higher: I blew it.

God: Well, that's no big surprise.

Jr. higher: Yeah, but this time I really blew it.

God: Tell me about it.

Jr. higher: I cheated on a test in school.

God: Goodness! Well, you're forgiven, but you'll have to pay the price.

71

Jr. higher:	Yeah, I know. I already told my teacher. She was glad I told her, but I'm still getting an F.		SCENE 3

Jr. higher: Yeah, I know. I already told my teacher. She was glad I told her, but I'm still getting an F.

God: No, I didn't mean that price. I mean, now you're in the doghouse for two weeks.

Jr. higher: The doghouse?

God: Yeah, that's what we call it up here when I won't have anything to do with you for awhile.

Jr. higher: But I thought I was forgiven.

God: Sure, for the cheating thing. But you'd have to expect that this would make me love you a little less. And it takes some time to earn that love back again.

Jr. higher: Oh. Well, see you in a couple weeks then.

God: If you're good.

Jr. higher: God?

God: I'm here. I'm <u>always</u> here.

Jr. higher: I messed up big-time.

God: Yeah, I know.

Jr. higher: I swore at my friend today.

God: Yeah, I know.

Jr. higher: Can you forgive me?

God: Of course I can—and I do.

Jr. higher: Is that it?

God: Well, I think it would probably be a good idea to ask for forgiveness from your friend, too.

Jr. higher: Yeah, I figured I should do that.

God: I love you.

Jr. higher: Even though I messed up?

God: My love for you has nothing to do with how good or bad you are.

Jr. higher: Thanks, God.

God: I'm glad you talked to me.

END

it again, with an oath: "I don't know the

...le while, those standing there went up to ...id, "Surely you are one of them, for your ...you away."

...egan to call down curses on himself and ...hem, "I don't know the man!"

...ly a rooster crowed. Then Peter remem-...rd Jesus had spoken: "Before the rooster ...ill disown me three times." And he went ...vept bitterly.

...on't be alarmed," he said. "You are ...looking for Jesus the Nazarene, who ...was crucified. He has risen! He is not ...place where they laid him. But go, tell his ...Peter, 'He is going ahead of you into ...you will see him just as he told you.'"

...days Peter stood up among the believers ...numbering about a hundred and twenty) ...d, "Brothers, the Scripture had to be ful-...e Holy Spirit spoke long ago through the ...d concerning Judas, who served as guide ...arrested Jesus."

...Peter stood up with the Eleven, raised ...voice and addressed the crowd: "Fellow ...ws and all of you who live in Jerusalem, ...n this to you; listen carefully to what I

Samantha, the Water Woman

The woman at the well, on racism

Bible passage: John 4:4-26, 39-42

GOALS

Students will—
- *Learn how to identify racism in their own lives.*
- *Identify one small step they can take this week to move beyond racism.*

JUMP START

New Prejudices

This is a tough subject. Almost all of us have some prejudices, some racism. Before you begin preparing this lesson, you may want to ask God to reveal your own prejudices to you—otherwise this will be a particularly tough lesson to teach. Many junior highers are unable or unwilling to admit their racism and prejudice simply because this country's media-defined youth culture says it's uncool to be racist. Racism is consequently buried in many junior highers. You might as well expect them to admit that they like to watch "Bass Fishing Masters."

So this first exercise is an attempt to air out the idea that most prejudices are, after all, ridiculous stereotypes.

Make sure you've copied and cut apart enough **New Prejudices game slips** (page 79) for everyone before the meeting. At this point in the lesson, hand out the slips, one per student.

You'll need—
- *New Prejudices game slips (page 79)*

Say to your group: These are "new prejudices," and we're going to put them into practice right now in our room.

Tell them to keep their instructions secret. However, also tell them that as they observe others treating people the same way *they're* treating people, they might want to move over and stand with them.

You'll notice, of course, that the four sets of instructions all say the same thing, verbatim ("Don't like anyone who has a hair color different from yours"). *Don't reveal this to the kids*—let them figure it out for themselves. Or tell them at the end of the exercise.

Now have your group stand up and begin milling

A note about the suitability of this activity to your group:

This exercise assumes at least some variety of hair color among the kids in your group. If your kids are ethnically homogeneous, you may need to use a different set of instructions, which you can simply write out and photocopy to replace the given instructions. Some alternatives:
- I don't like you if you go to a different school than me.
- I don't like you if you're wearing a different style of shoe than I'm wearing (tennis shoes, sandals, boots, wingtips).
- I don't like you if you're not in the same grade as me.

 he was another one of the outsiders that Jesus seemed to spend most of his time with. She was female, she was several times divorced, and she was living with her lover. She was also Samaritan. And Jews, St. John reminded us in his Gospel, "do not associate with Samaritans." Think of a white person in 1955 boarding a Birmingham bus, then moving all the way to the back, sitting down next to a black, and starting a conversation. That's what Jesus, a Jew, did with this Samaritan woman.

around, putting their new prejudices into action. Allow this to continue for a few minutes—you be the judge on when it's time to stop. Then have everyone return to their seats.

Ask your group:
- *What are some of your reactions to what we just did?*
- *How did you feel about turning your back on people for such a stupid reason?*
- *How do you think real prejudices start?*
- *What's it mean to assume something?*

Then say to your group: We're going to try something else that might teach us a little about assuming.

Assume Away

Ask for a student to volunteer, then have him or her leave the room (preferably with another adult).

Then ask the remaining students a list of questions about the volunteer student that only close friends of the volunteer would know. Call on students to offer answers—but never students who are friends of the volunteer. Consequently, most of the answers you'll get will be speculation and assumption, albeit well-meaning.

Some sample questions:

Be cautious here. On one hand, it's good to get assumptions out on the table. But it's a delicate task when your youth group includes members of a community or race being used as an example in the discussion. It can be done safely, but only by monitoring the discussion carefully. Otherwise the typical statements will come up—Jewish people are rich, Mexicans are lazy, blacks are athletic—that may hurt even though such myths are merely reported by the kids, objectively and with no malice.

- *What's this person's favorite flavor of ice cream?*
- *Favorite TV show?*
- *Favorite musician or group?*
- *Favorite color?*
- *Middle name?*
- *Hobby?*

Call the volunteer back into the room. Ask the questions one at a time and give the answer previously given. Then ask for the real answer.

When you're done, ask the volunteer how it felt to have people assuming those answers about her.

Then ask your group:
- *How is this like prejudice or racism? (racism is basically about making assumptions)*
- *What are some assumptions that people make about other races?*
- *How do you think God feels about racism?* **[There is no scriptural basis for any kind of racism, and it is in direct contrast with the character of God]**

GETTING THE POINT
Equations

Say to your group: Time for an algebra lesson.

Then write this equation on the board or overhead:

IF A = B, AND B = C, THEN A = C

Explain that algebra is all about equations. It involves figuring out the value of the missing parts of an equation and how the different parts relate to each other. Further explain this equation by saying (and writing),

IF 10 PENNIES = 1 DIME, AND 1 DIME = 2 NICKELS, THEN 10 PENNIES = 2 NICKELS

Say to your group: We can use the same idea—equations—to help us find our prejudices.

Explain that racism isn't always outright hatred—it can be just making wrong assumptions.

Use one of the assumption statements mentioned in the box at the left. Write the statement in equation form:

IF JUAN = MEXICAN, AND MEXICANS = LAZY, THEN JUAN = LAZY

Explain that this shows how racism works. When we make assumptions about anyone based on their race or color, or assumptions about a whole group of people based on their race or color, we are being racist.

Say something like this to your group: Research shows that there is a disproportionate level of alcoholism among Native Americans, for a variety of reasons. This is not racism. But it is racism to say, "Jim is a Native American—he must be an alcoholic" or "All Native Americans are alcoholics." Such statements are based on assumption.

Try this equation method with a couple more statements. Explain again that the issue is our assumptions. Any time we make assumptions about another person based on their race or color (among other things), we are being racist.

Samantha and Jesus

Tell your kids you're going to help them look at a familiar Bible story in a new way. Don't explain anything else at this point.

You'll need—
- *Bibles*
- *copies of Samantha and Jesus (page 80)*
- *pens or pencils*

Have everyone turn their Bibles to John 4:4-26, 39-42. Read the passage to your students while they follow along. Make sure you've read the passage yourself several times before the lesson so you can read it with clarity and drama.

After you've finished...

Ask your group: Does anyone have any idea what this passage has to do with racism?

A couple of kids might know that the answer lies in the fact that Jesus was a Jew, and the woman at the well was a Samaritan.

If your students don't know this, don't hand it to them yet. Instead do one of three things (choose the option that best suits your group's junior highers and their predictable response to the different types of teaching exercises):

- **Option 1.** Pass out copies of **Samantha and Jesus** (page 80) and pens or pencils to each student and have them work on their own to circle answers before you discuss them.
- **Option 2.** Read the questions aloud while your students read along on their own sheets, then have them circle an answer before you give them the correct answer.
- **Option 3.** Ignore this Wild Page altogether, and just read the questions aloud, having your students yell out the letter of their answer ("b!...c!...a!").

Here are the correct answers:

1. c	5. b	9. a
2. a	6. a	10. c
3. b	7. c	11. c
4. c	8. b	

FAST FORWARD

Obliterating Racism in the Junior High World

Ask your students to brainstorm actions that junior highers can take to overcome racial prejudice. Suggest that these will be most effective if they're little ideas, not huge ideas. Write all reasonable ideas on your whiteboard, chalkboard, or overhead projector. Some possibilities:

- Saying hi to someone of another race, especially a race you're not comfortable around.
- Praying that God would help you see the racism in your life.
- Developing a friendship with someone of another race.
- Not laughing at, or otherwise discouraging, racist jokes.

After a good list is in place, pass out copies of **Overcoming Racism** (page 81). Have students write down the second half of the sentence for themselves. Then have a few kids share what they wrote.

Close your time by asking God to heal our country of the problem of racism, and asking God to heal us of the racism in our own lives.

> **You'll need—**
> - *copies of* **Overcoming Racism** *(page 81)*
> - *pens or pencils*
> - *whiteboard, chalkboard, or overhead projector*

NEW PREJUDICES

game slips

Instructions for leader: A glance at the four prejudices below will tell you that they're actually all the same prejudice—*but don't let your students know that.* In fact, you might go so far as to use four or more colors of paper for the slips—anything to give the illusion that there are *several* prejudices floating around the room, not just one. For directions on how to play, see page 75.

✂

PREJUDICE 1

You can't stand people who don't have the same hair color as you. In fact you aren't comfortable even being in the same room as them. When you *have* to be in the same room with them (as you have to be now), you still refuse to stand within 10 feet of them, refuse to talk with them, and refuse to even make eye contact with them. And in particular, you don't let them see you looking at their hair.

PREJUDICE 2

You can't stand people who don't have the same hair color as you. In fact you aren't comfortable even being in the same room as them. When you *have* to be in the same room with them (as you have to be now), you still refuse to stand within 10 feet of them, refuse to talk with them, and refuse to even make eye contact with them. And in particular, you don't let them see you looking at their hair.

PREJUDICE 3

You can't stand people who don't have the same hair color as you. In fact you aren't comfortable even being in the same room as them. When you *have* to be in the same room with them (as you have to be now), you still refuse to stand within 10 feet of them, refuse to talk with them, and refuse to even make eye contact with them. And in particular, you don't let them see you looking at their hair.

PREJUDICE 4

You can't stand people who don't have the same hair color as you. In fact you aren't comfortable even being in the same room as them. When you *have* to be in the same room with them (as you have to be now), you still refuse to stand within 10 feet of them, refuse to talk with them, and refuse to even make eye contact with them. And in particular, you don't let them see you looking at their hair.

SAMANTHA AND JESUS

Find the answers to these questions in John 4:4-26, 39-42.

1. **What country was Jesus walking through?**
   a. Samary-town
   b. Samurai
   c. Samaria

2. **Why did Jesus stop at the well?**
   a. because he was thirsty
   b. to meet someone
   c. to offer a sacrifice

3. **Why did the woman approach the well?**
   a. so Jesus could heal her
   b. to get water
   c. to throw in a coin for good luck

4. **Where were Jesus' disciples?**
   a. at a massive party
   b. they were with him
   c. in town getting food

5. **What nationality was the woman?**
   a. it doesn't say
   b. Samaritan
   c. Jewish

6. **What did Jesus first ask the woman?**
   a. "Can I have some water?"
   b. "Are you a Samaritan?"
   c. "Where'd you get those awesome sandals?"

7. **Why was the woman freaked that Jesus spoke to her?**
   a. she didn't see him there
   b. she was a nut-case
   c. Jews and Samaritans never spoke to each other

8. **Why didn't Jews and Samaritans "associate" with each other?**
   a. they didn't like each other's food
   b. they hated each other and were completely racist about each other
   c. God told them they shouldn't hang out together

9. **What did Jesus offer her?**
   a. salvation
   b. a new pail to draw water with
   c. a great deal on a used donkey

10. **Why was this such a big deal?**
    a. no Samaritans had ever been saved before
    b. Jesus had never spoken to a Samaritan before
    c. Jesus ignored the racist traditions of his people

11. **If you could summarize what Jesus would say about racism, based on what you've seen here, it would probably be this:**
    a. "I'd prefer it if people weren't racist"
    b. "If it's not too uncomfortable for you, it would be good to overcome racism"
    c. "Racism has no place in a Christian's life and should be dealt with as serious sin"

WILDPAGE

OVERCOMING RACISM

I will take one step toward overcoming any racism in me by taking the following action this week:

WILDPAGE

OVERCOMING RACISM

I will take one step toward overcoming any racism in me by taking the following action this week:

WILDPAGE

OVERCOMING RACISM

I will take one step toward overcoming any racism in me by taking the following action this week:

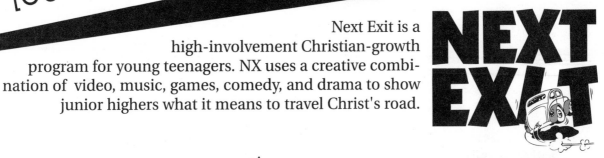

[OUR NAME IS THE AGE]

10 TO 20 produces event programming and products for students aged 10 to 20. Our writers, artists, producers and presenters are bound by a common passion: to present the Gospel to teenagers in the most effective, creative, powerful ways possible. Contact us for event booking information or product orders.

live-media show for junior highers

Next Exit is a high-involvement Christian-growth program for young teenagers. NX uses a creative combination of video, music, games, comedy, and drama to show junior highers what it means to travel Christ's road.

Change-Up!

evangelism training for high school students   Face to face, friend to friend, nothing conveys the Gospel more effectively than one teenager to another. Change-Up! shows your students how. Co-produced by Youth For Christ/USA.

live television for teenagers   Not For Broadcast is a live comedy talk-show with a message . . . *in fast-forward.* From show open to closing credits, NFB allows your audience to see and share the thrill of living for Jesus.

Custom Programs

conference production and presentation   10 TO 20 assists event producers in all aspects of youth conference programming: writing, development, video production, directing, and custom presentations.

what kids want to read
10 TO 20 Press produces positive books and products that teenagers enjoy reading, including *Wild Truth Journal, Cheap Thrills* and *Outrageous Dates.*

P·R·E·S·S

10 TO 20 • Box 604 • Del Mar, CA 92014 • 619 793-8275

YOUTH SPECIALTIES TITLES

Professional Resources

Developing Spiritual Growth in Junior High Students
Developing Student Leaders
Equipped to Serve: Volunteer Youth Worker Training
  Course
Help! I'm a Sunday School Teacher!
Help! I'm a Volunteer Youth Worker!
How to Expand Your Youth Ministry
How to Recruit and Train Volunteer Youth Workers
The Ministry of Nurture
One Kid at a Time: Reaching Youth Through Mentoring
Peer Counseling in Youth Groups
Advanced Peer Counseling in Youth Groups

Discussion Starter Resources

Get 'Em Talking
4th-6th Grade TalkSheets
High School TalkSheets
Junior High TalkSheets
High School TalkSheets: Psalms and Proverbs
Junior High TalkSheets: Psalms and Proverbs
More High School TalkSheets
More Junior High TalkSheets
Parent Ministry TalkSheets
What If...? 450 Thought-Provoking Questions to Get
  Teenagers Talking, Thinking, Doing
Would You Rather...? 465 Provacative Questions to Get
  Kids Talking

Ideas Library

Combos: 1-4, 5-8, 9-12, 13-16, 17-20, 21-24, 25-28, 29-32,
  33-36, 37-40, 41-44, 45-48, 49-52, 53-56
Ideas Index

Youth Ministry Programming

Compassionate Kids: Practical Ways to Involve Kids in
  Mission and Service
Creative Bible Lessons in John: Encounters with Jesus
Creative Bible Lessons in Romans: Faith on Fire!
Creative Bible Lessons on the Life of Christ
Creative Junior High Programs from A to Z, Vol. 1 (A-M)
Creative Programming Ideas for Junior High Ministry
Dramatic Pauses
Facing Your Future: Graduating Youth Groups with a
  Faith that Lasts
Great Fundraising Ideas for Youth Groups

More Great Fundraising Ideas for Youth Groups
Great Retreats for Youth Groups
Greatest Skits on Earth
Greatest Skits on Earth, Vol. 2
Hot Illustrations for Youth Talks
Memory Makers
More Hot Illustrations for Youth Talks
Incredible Questionnaires for Youth Ministry
Junior High Game Nights
More Junior High Game Nights
Play It! Great Games for Groups
Play It Again! More Great Games for Groups
Road Trip
Spontaneous Melodramas
Super Sketches for Youth Ministry
Teaching the Bible Creatively
Up Close and Personal: How to Build Community in Your
  Youth Group
Worship Services for Youth Groups

Clip Art

ArtSource Vol. 1—Fantastic Activities
ArtSource Vol. 2—Borders, Symbols, Holidays, and
  Attention Getters
ArtSource Vol. 3—Sports
ArtSource Vol. 4—Phrases and Verses
ArtSource Vol. 5—Amazing Oddities and Appalling
  Images
ArtSource Vol. 6—Spiritual Topics
ArtSource Vol. 7—Variety Pack
ArtSource CD-ROM (contains Volumes 1-7)

Videos

Edge TV
God Views
The Heart of Youth Ministry: A Morning with Mike
  Yaconelli
Next Time I Fall in Love Video Curriculum
Understanding Your Teenager Video Curriculum
Witnesses

Student Books

Grow For It Journal
Grow For It Journal through the Scriptures
Wild Truth Journal for Junior Highers